IF TREES COULD TALK

LIFE LESSONS FROM THE WISDOM OF THE WOODS

HOLLY WORTON

TRIBAL PUBLISHING

Trees are sanctuaries. Whoever knows how to speak to them, whoever knows how to listen to them, can learn the truth. . . . Whoever has learned how to listen to trees no longer wants to be a tree. He wants to be nothing except what he is. That is home. That is happiness.

— Herman Hesse

CONTENTS

If Trees Could Talk:
Life Lessons from the Wisdom of the Woods

Holly Worton

Published by Tribal Publishing Ltd

www.hollyworton.com

ISBN 978-1-911161-24-0

ACKNOWLEDGMENTS

Writing this book was much more challenging than I imagined when I started this project. I had been working on my first novel, and putting that on the back burner to focus on a book about the stories of trees seemed much easier. In reality, this project stretched me outside my comfort zone and helped me to grow in ways I didn't anticipate.

First and foremost, I will be eternally grateful to A.O. for introducing me to the world of spirituality, which has added a whole new layer to my life's experience. My heart has so much more to say, but it feels as though putting it into words might limit the depth of all that you have given me. Thank you, thank you, thank you.

To Vickie Young and my Records Keepers: thank you for being the ones who introduced me to the world of communicating with trees. Vickie, it was your magical Weekly Messages that got me started, and this book wouldn't have existed without that one email that changed my world. Thank you.

To the Newlands Corner Yew: I've already thanked you

in person, but I need to say once more that this book wouldn't exist if it weren't for you. Thank you, once again, for gifting me the idea for this project.

Thanks also to all the trees who chose to participate in this book. I know I've already thanked you all individually, but I need to say it again here: thank you for helping me to make this project a reality. Your stories were so very beautiful.

Thanks to Gary and Olga of the Forest Bathing and Nature Therapy Meetup group for guiding me on my first forest bathing experience and for introducing me to the magical yew grove at Newlands Corner. The spark of life that became this book was ignited on that afternoon.

Naomi Darlington, who has joined me on many walks through the woods, is a talented and accurate transcriber. Thank you, Naomi, for taking my audio files — often of very poor quality, with the wind whipping around me as I spoke — and turning them into coherent transcriptions. It was always such a pleasure to see your emails pop into my inbox with the latest tree stories.

Massive thanks to my Mastergut group for helping me to stay on track and for lifting me up when things got difficult. Thank you for always reminding me to listen to my gut and not my head. Cara, Cathy, and Joanna: you three are a massive support, and I love our bimonthly calls. I also learn so much from your channeling: you're all so different in the way that you work, and I am so grateful for your example.

Thanks to Lisa Wechtenhiser for your channeled guidance, coaching, and support over the years. Most of all, thanks for teaching me about unwavering trust. I've come a long way, and I'm still working on it!

To Sara O'Dowd, creator of the magical The Haven at Avebury B&B, where I spent several nights throughout the course of creating this book: thank you for all the wonderful conversations, thank you for all you have taught me, and thank you for the magical retreat you created at The Haven. I will miss it dearly. The concepts that you taught me opened me up to receive and to understand many of the stories from the trees.

Massive thanks to Suneet Goomer, who first introduced me to the concept of spirit guides, and who is now teaching me about how to work with the spirits of the plants for deep, deep healing. I am thrilled to be learning from you this year on the Plant Spirit Healing Apprenticeship. Your work is truly life-changing.

Many thanks to OBOD — The Order of Bards, Ovates & Druids — for helping me to refine my spiritual path as it relates to the magic of Nature. I learned so much on the Bardic Grade, and I can't wait to delve even deeper on the Ovate Grade. The magic of Awen has truly inspired this book.

Thanks to my family — my father and my grandmother were avid gardeners, and their example sparked in me a love for plants — and to my parents, who have always been supportive of my life's adventures, even when they led me thousands of miles away from home. Thanks for always being there for me, and thanks for giving me my first patch of earth in the garden.

To Fred and Virginia Siegel, thanks for hiring me for the best first job ever at Mountaire Garden Supply back when I was fifteen years old. I have such fond memories of working there in the summers, and I learned so much about flowers, plants, and trees. It truly helped me to deepen my relationship with the plant world, and every year when summer comes around, I am reminded of Mountaire.

Finally, last but certainly not least, massive thanks to Agustín: not just my perfect partner in life and in business, but also an excellent developmental editor. Thanks for your endless support in everything I do, and eternal thanks for helping me to embark on a path of healing so I could step into my true self, which apparently involves conversing with trees.

PART I

INTRODUCTION

I remember exactly when I first began talking to trees: it was in May 2015. A couple of years prior, I had started getting weekly Akashic Records emails from my friend Vickie Young, and it was one of her messages that sparked a new chapter in my life and ultimately led to the creation of this project. The Akashic Records are an extensive library of energetic records of all souls, including their past, present, and possible future lives. It includes all events, thoughts, words, emotions, and intentions ever to have occurred in these past, present, or possible future lives. It's like an archive of each person throughout all their lifetimes. It is thought that each soul has its own Records, like a set of encyclopedias where each book in the set represents a single lifetime. It's the history — and future — of you, as a soul.

These Records can be quickly and easily accessed in a variety of different ways. There are plenty of training programs available online, and author Linda Howe shares in her books a simple prayer that she uses to access the

Records. That's how I first learned to access the Akashic Records myself, and it's how I continue to do so today.

Even though I know how to access my own Records, I rarely take the time to do it, which is why I greatly value the weekly messages that I get from Vickie. They're short and focused, and they often provide a starting point for my journaling and mindset work each week. I've been getting them on and off since 2013, and they're a very important part of my personal development work. On this particular week, back in May 2015, I received the following message from Vickie and my Records Keepers:

> *This week Holly, when you are on your sacred walks, take a moment and listen to the plant spirits. They have so much to tell you and they want to share with you their knowledge of the medicine that plant people have for you and for others.*
>
> *Hold your hands on a tree (you know, The Tree!) and just listen for a voice in an unexpected way. Feel the energy of the tree and notice how it is waking up and moving inside. Feel the energy of the tree inside of your body and notice that a chakra stirs up.*
>
> *Notice this on each plant that you hold. You see...each plant that you come in contact with will have a healthy influence and message for you. All you have to do is listen and believe!*

To be honest, I was a bit skeptical when I read this email. "Me? Talk to trees? I don't know how to do that," I thought. But later that week, when I went on my weekly Nature walk, I had the opportunity to give it a try when I got lost in the woods. In fact, I got lost so many times, I turned an 11.6 mile (18.6 km) walk into a 16.7 mile (26.8 km) walk. I was on a route from Milford to Haslemere in Surrey, England, and I was following the directions that I had printed out. I didn't have a map with me, which was not unusual at the time because, at this point in my life, I often went walking without a map. Later, I would go on to do more training in outdoors leadership and navigation, and I became much more careful on my walks: always walking with a paper map and compass for navigation, with the OS Maps app on my phone as a backup.

But back in 2015, I was a bit reckless. I did most of my walking in the lowlands of Surrey, which always felt like a safe environment to wander around in. Unlike in the hills of California — where I grew up — in Surrey, there were no bears, mountain lions, or rattlesnakes to worry about. It always felt relatively harmless, which had led me to put caution to the side when I went out walking.

Before I got lost for the first time that day, I remembered my weekly message from the Records Keepers, and I stopped to connect with the trees. I walked up to one at random, and I put my hands on its bark. I immediately heard the message: "It's okay." The words sounded clearly in my head, in a calm, male voice. I remembered to focus on my chakras, as the message from my Records Keepers had suggested, and I felt movement in my throat center as the energy shifted. It made sense that my fifth chakra would be activated, as I was focusing on communication with the trees. The fifth energy center, or throat chakra, is the one that's related to communication and expression.

I was confused by the tree's message: "It's okay." What did that mean? That was all the tree had to say to me, and at that point, I didn't understand what it meant. I assumed that I must have gotten something wrong, and that I was missing another part of the message. After all, I was new to this tree communication thing. I went to another tree, hoping to get more information, but it repeated the same message, albeit in a different male voice. Once again, I felt movement in my throat chakra. It was as though new avenues of communication were stirring within me, yet I couldn't understand what the trees were actually trying to tell me.

Their message wasn't clear (or so I thought), but I resolved to continue on my walk and try again later. I assumed that because I was new at tree communication, I either wasn't getting the full details, or I didn't understand the words I had been given. However, I would soon understand that "It's okay" was all I needed to hear for me to know exactly what action to take next.

Walking along a dirt trail through a wood, I noticed that it appeared to be a commercial forest. The trail was deeply grooved in places where heavy load vehicles had left their mark, and the woodland was made up of a sea of identical conifers. I don't usually like walking through such places, as they feel strange and unnatural to me, but it was a beautiful day, and I felt light-hearted and joyful as I explored the new route. I continued uphill along the trail, soon coming out of the wood into an open area full of low-growing heather, yellow flowering gorse, and lush green bracken. Consulting my printed directions, I turned left. Unfortunately, I hadn't clearly identified where I was on the page as it compared to where I actually was on the trail, and I turned left where I should have continued on the main path as it curved around to the right, eventually turning left further on.

I happily continued straight down the trail until it closely approached the noisy A3 road and turned right. This is where I realized I was lost. When I attempted to retrace my steps, I got even more lost. I hadn't seen another walker in over an hour, and there was no one around I could ask for directions...or so I thought.

I was on open access land, which meant that there were many little trails going off in all directions, and no public footpath signs to be found. I had no idea where I was or how to get back on track, and I felt really confused. This is probably the point in the story where I should explain that I have high functioning autism — formerly known as Aspergers — and if I don't make a conscious, focused effort to stay calm in emergency situations I can often spiral into a meltdown. When that happens, all common sense goes out the window and I panic. I could feel myself heading toward a meltdown as I struggled to figure out where exactly I was and where I needed to go to get back on the right path.

A simple phrase popped into my mind: "It's okay." I remembered what the trees had said just a few minutes prior, and at last, their message made sense. Everything *was* okay. I just needed a little help to get me back on track. I went up to a slender young birch tree and put my hands on its trunk. I asked it where I needed to go to get back on track, and it gave me a very clear answer. It told me which direction I needed to start off in, and where I needed to turn left, then left again to get back on the main trail.

The birch was right, of course. From there, I quickly and easily got back on the right track, and I soon found my way out of confusion and back onto the route I had been following. I felt fantastic: the solution had been so simple! I was so grateful for the guidance that I thanked the trees out loud as I walked. I was also thankful that it was a weekday, and there were no other walkers in sight to hear me as I spontaneously and effusively thanked the forest for its knowledge. It was almost unbelievable how I had gone from total disorientation to absolute knowing, thanks to the simple instructions from the birch.

A new chapter in my life had begun.

This experience gave me a new awareness of the trees that I passed as I went on my walks: they had wisdom that I could easily access by simply striking up a conversation and asking them a question. Yet it wasn't until almost three years later — in January 2018, when I was on a Forest Bathing and Nature Therapy Meetup — that I deepened my connection with the trees even further. After a delightful afternoon of smelling, tasting, and engaging in completely new ways with the forest at Newlands Corner in Surrey, the group was guided to enter an ancient grove of yew trees. We were told to select one of the trees and then connect with it.

I instantly knew which one I needed to work with: it was a yew that had caught my eye off to the right-hand side of where we were standing in the grove. I walked straight to the yew, and I put my hands on its bark to make first contact. I then leaned in to hug the tree as I greeted it. I felt an instant connection to the yew, and he immediately began to speak to me.

The ancient yew acknowledged that he knew I was having trouble with the novel I had been working on at the time, my first work of fiction. It was slow moving, a struggle: I had always found writing nonfiction books to be easy, but fiction was a whole other story. I was learning a new skill, and it was very slow going and not at all fun. The yew suggested that I set aside the novel and instead, write a different book: a book of tree stories, in which I would connect with trees in the same way that I was connecting with him, and they would share their stories with me.

"This is your work," the yew said, "to share our wisdom."

He made it clear to me that it was my job to help people connect to Nature, and to help rebuild the love and respect that humanity used to have for the Earth. He said that this was the way of the future; that this was one way to help the environment. It wasn't enough to conserve water and other resources; humanity needed to rebuild its relationship with Nature. He said that this book would be a piece in the puzzle of what was necessary to help rekindle the deep and healthy relationship that humanity once had with Nature.

The yew acknowledged that I might need to "wrap it in a package" that would make the stories easier for people to digest: that perhaps the book would need to be marketed as fiction so that it could reach a wider audience. Many truths can be shared in fiction, and he suggested that perhaps the tree stories would be better received by readers if they thought they were made up. Or that maybe it would need to be marketed as a children's book: he reminded me of the Madeleine L'Engle quote "You have to write the book that wants to be written. And if the book will be too difficult for grown-ups, then you write it for children."

I took his advice and toyed around with the idea of writing this book as fiction: an eleven-year-old girl goes into the forest and gets one story from each of the Ogam trees. The Ogam — often spelled Ogham — is an early alphabet that has been identified as the earliest written record of the old Irish language. The original alphabet was comprised of twenty letters, with a further five added at a later date. Now, it is sometimes used by druids and other pagan groups as a form of divination, with each letter symbolizing a tree, which in turn represents a message.

The twenty trees of the Ogam are birch, rowan, alder, willow, ash, hawthorn, oak, holly, hazel, apple, vine, ivy, reed, blackthorn, elder, silver fir, gorse, heather, poplar, and yew. My idea all sounded very neat and tidy, quite unlike how this book turned out.

In this initial plan, I would enter the woods myself, collecting the stories, and I would put it all together as if it were a novel. I suspected that the yew was right, and this might help the book to reach a wider audience: that of people who were open to the concept of tree-talk but in a magical, fictional setting. Not everyone will accept the idea of a person who talks to trees, and the yew had made it very clear to me that it was important for me to help them by bringing their stories to the widest possible audience of readers.

Yet presenting this as a work of fiction didn't quite feel right. I detest lying, and I'm extremely uncomfortable with half-truths. After months of going back and forth and worrying about what to do, I decided to simply tell the truth: yes, I talk to trees. Yes, these are their stories. No, this is *not* a work of fiction.

I wasn't fully comfortable with this decision, mostly because of my fears around what people would think of me. Throughout the year I found myself evading conversation around the topic of the book I was working on. I feared judgment, and only my closest friends knew the full truth of the contents of this book. Yet I knew that this was the right thing for me to do: I had to be honest about exactly where these stories had come from.

Because, let's be honest: whether or not you believe that people can actually talk to trees — and hear their replies — there's a lot more power to these messages if you know the truth of this book, which is that the stories were actually given to me by the trees. I didn't make this stuff up. It isn't a work of fiction. This is real. This is my truth, my experience, and I have chosen to share the unfiltered stories with you, just as they were given to me.

As I went on my weekly walks in Nature, various trees started to speak out to me: "*I'm in your book*," some of them would inform me. If it was a cold or wet day, I would make a mental note to return and collect their story. Sometimes, if the weather was good, I would sit right down against the trunk of the tree and immediately connect with it to receive its tale. Several times throughout the year, it occurred to me that perhaps I should travel further from home to connect with some of the "superstar" trees in Britain: the most famous, ancient and gnarled trees that make their way into books and magazines. I thought of the Fortingall Yew, the Llangernyw Yew, and the Big Belly Oak of Savernake Forest. But that didn't feel right: according to the Newlands Corner Yew, *all* trees have a story, and I had such an abundance of trees who were willing to share their wisdom with me that I decided to stick with the trees I knew. After all, I already had a relationship with them.

And this was a very important part of the journey of creating this book: building a relationship with the trees. While I've always loved trees for their beauty — as a child, I absolutely loved eating broccoli because I thought it looked like little green trees — I began to connect with them on a much deeper level, as individuals. I learned to think of them in the way I think of the different people in my life, and I started to feel like I knew them.

This wasn't an easy process, though. Just because I was given a very clear topic for the book doesn't mean that collecting the stories was a walk in the park (pun absolutely intended). Instead, it triggered all of my insecurities. Though I've been talking to trees since 2015, and I've been channeling spirit guides since the year before that, this book stretched me out of my comfort zone and forced me to grow both as a person and as a channel. Channeling is how I can best describe the method I used to collect these stories: it involves opening up a connection or line of communication, often to unseen or nonphysical beings such as spirit guides, angels, or ascended masters. You can channel your Higher Self, and you can also channel Nature spirits, such as the spirits of the trees who shared their stories in this book.

This book became a personal lesson in *I am good enough*, something that I've struggled with my entire life. It's the theme that keeps coming up over and over when I do mindset work with myself to my clear fears, blocks, and limiting beliefs. I believe it's one of the main topics that my soul chose to work on, develop, and clear in this lifetime. It's one of the primary subjects in my personal school of life.

It didn't help that the stories weren't what I had expected: I thought I would receive a series of quaint and magical fairy tales, and what I actually got was very different...so much so that I worried that the stories might be a little too serious. I also struggled with the fear that my channeling skills weren't good enough for me to receive the *full* tales, but rather only a superficial version of them...and that there was actually much more underneath the surface than I was able to tap into. The Newlands Corner Yew had given me a very serious task, and I wanted to do justice to the trees' project. And to do so, I needed to believe that I was good enough to make it happen.

1

WHERE I'M COMING FROM

Before we delve into the stories of the trees, I thought it might be useful for you to get an idea of where I'm coming from. The previous chapter probably left you with a series of questions: *How is it that trees can talk? How do I hear them? How is this possible? Is this for real?* When I first became familiar with the idea of tree communication, I had a lot of questions, and it wasn't until I experienced it for myself that I learned how it all worked...at least, how it worked for *me*. I'm sure everyone who talks to trees has their own way of going about it.

Here's how I see the world: everything has a spirit. Not just people, but also animals, plants, and minerals. The official term for this belief is animism, and it is common in many pagan belief systems, including those of many indigenous peoples. It's a way of being that makes me feel very connected to everything around me, particularly the elements of Nature and the members of the plant, animal, and mineral realms.

This means that when I'm talking to a tree, I'm not talking to its bark or its branches, or its leaves — I'm actually communicating with its spirit. This is the same as the way that we do not talk to the skin, the limbs, or the hair of another human being — we communicate with their spirit, their soul, the energy that brings their body to life. Sometimes I'll speak out loud to a tree, but most of the time I'm "speaking" with my mind: sending silent thoughts of communication directly to the tree spirit. And when I "hear" the tree responding to me, what I hear is their words flowing into my mind. It's a kind of silent, telepathic communication.

For the purposes of this book, I channeled the trees' stories directly. This means that I used myself as a verbal channel to receive and speak the trees' stories out loud into my phone, which I then had transcribed for this book. When I do this, it's as though my own consciousness moves to the back of my mind and the tree's spirit takes the driver's seat. I'm still there, but I'm a passive observer in the background: watching, listening, but not interfering. I felt that this would be a much more straightforward way of capturing the trees' messages and, even more importantly, the essence and the energy of their stories. It was also much easier to speak their words than to write them down directly, as I would have struggled to keep up the pace with their messages, which were often passionate and ranting. Finally, it allowed me to truly *feel* the energy of each tree as it was speaking through me — an experience that was often exhilarating and deeply moving.

For some readers, who are familiar with the concept of channeling, this will all seem perfectly normal. For others — perhaps for most readers — it might be a stretch outside their current belief system. If this is the case for you, I would like to encourage you to open your mind to the possibility that trees *can* talk. Wherever you are on the spectrum of belief, if you keep an open mind, I assure you that you'll get something out of this book. If this is too much of a stretch for you to believe, then I suggest that you simply take this book as a work of fiction, not nonfiction, and in this way you can still get the value from the stories of the trees.

In any case, I invite you to set aside any judgment you might be feeling. If we allow our inner critic to take a back seat, as my mind does when I'm channeling, we open up space for new things that are waiting to be discovered by us. And in turn, we expand our awareness to include new worlds of possibilities.

As you read this book, you'll notice that I refer to certain trees as "he" or "she." When I first started talking to trees, I always heard a male voice in my head. Each tree seemed to have a different voice, much like different human beings do, but they were all male. Eventually, I began to make contact with trees that had a female voice, such as a holly tree that I connected with during a plant spirit initiation ceremony guided by my friend Suneet.

In this book, the vast majority of the trees had male voices, with the most notable exceptions being The Grandmothers, The Three Witches, and the Savernake Queen Oak. I'm not sure why this is, and I'm not sure if it's even important whether the voices are male or female. In any case, speaking from a botanical perspective, most trees and plants that will be familiar to the home gardener or the woodland walker are what's known as "monoecious," which means that a single plant or tree bears both male and female flowers. Beeches, oaks, and sycamores, for example, are monoecious, with both male and female flowers occurring on the same tree.

Other types of trees and plants are called "dioecious," which means that some trees produce male flowers, and other individuals produce female flowers. Hollies, for example, are dioecious, and you may notice when you're out for a walk during autumn and winter when the hollies are fruiting that only some will be adorned with red berries, while others will be barren. The berry-producing trees are the females — only female plants are able to set fruit and produce berries — and the plain green hollies are (probably) the males. If you pay attention when you're outdoors in areas where hollies tend to grow, you may see many more fruitless hollies than you will see fruit-bearing ones. This might be because there are more males along the trails that you're walking, or it may mean the exact opposite: that there aren't *any* male hollies in the area, as you need males and females near each other (within about 200 yards) so that the females can produce berries.

To give you another example, yews are mostly dioecious, but occasionally can be monoecious, and they can even change sex with time. The famous Fortingall Yew in Scotland, believed to be one of the oldest trees in Europe, recently surprised the world by appearing to change sex when it began producing red arils —the particular type of fruit this tree produces — on its upper branches. The yew had been male for as long as anyone could remember — the tree is thought to be at least 2,000 to 3,000 years old, though some estimate its age at 5,000 years — and it suddenly began behaving as though it were female.

Botany lessons aside, I don't think it really matters whether the tree spirits speak to me in a male or a female voice, and I don't think it's worth reading anything more into this. That's simply how I perceived the voices of the trees that chose to participate in this book. Perhaps we hear the voices that we need to hear, in the way that we need to hear them.

The important thing, as I see it, is that trees — whether male, female, or bisexual/hermaphroditic — have a much broader perspective on life than we humans do. Trees can live hundreds — even thousands — of years, compared to people, who for the most part don't live past the age of ninety or one hundred. As healthcare improves, our lives are lengthened, but our time on Earth is still very, very short compared to the lives of the trees. This, combined with the vast communication network that trees have, which you'll hear about in future chapters, means that trees have access to thousands and thousands of years of wisdom that we're able to tap into.

Nature is generally defined as the phenomena of the collective physical world on our planet, including the elements of the plant realm, the animal realm, and the mineral realm. It refers to the Earth's resources and to the four elements: earth, air, water, and fire. It concerns the features of the Earth, rather than things that have been created by humans. Because Nature is deeply sacred to me, I have chosen to reject conventional grammatical advice, and you will see that I capitalize the word "Nature" throughout this book. This was a conscious decision, made to emphasize the importance of Nature in my life, and in all our lives.

My own relationship with Nature has evolved greatly over the course of my life. My father and my grandmother were avid gardeners, and they were probably responsible for planting the seed of my love for Nature. When I was fourteen years old, my parents gave me a patch of dirt in the front yard for me to start my own garden. My dad took me down to a local garden center called Mountaire Garden Supply where Virginia, the owner's daughter, helped me to plan out my garden. One year later, when I was ready to look for my first job, it was she who hired me. For a young lover of Nature, this was the perfect job, and I learned so much about gardening and ornamental plants.

At the same time, I developed a great interest in walking and hiking. I lived just down the street from the Mt. Diablo State Park in Clayton, California, which is located across the bay from San Francisco. It was no more than ten minutes on foot from my house, which meant that I spent many a scorching hot summer afternoon exploring the trails with my friends, who were surprisingly willing to be dragged up the mountain by me. When I went to university, my passion for hiking and exploring sadly waned, which was especially unfortunate considering that the hills surrounding San Luis Obispo were filled with gorgeous places to walk. However, my passion for gardening was rekindled each summer when I returned to work at Mountaire.

From there, I spent many years in Latin America. I lived for several years on the coast in southeast Mexico, where I cultivated tropical plants in my spare time, of which I didn't have much. I lived in the jungle, surrounded by lush Nature, but I didn't really have the time to take advantage of it, aside from admiring its beauty every day. After living in Argentina, and spending much time in Chile, I moved to London, then to the Surrey Hills, an area rich in public footpaths and emerald green forests. Surrey is the most wooded county in England, which means that I have had an abundance of trails to explore under the shade of trees.

I began exploring the local trails on a regular basis, and I eventually ventured out on some of the longer National Trails, experiences which I shared in my books on the South Downs Way and The Ridgeway. I was walking, walking, walking through the woods, but I wasn't really *connecting* with Nature. At the same time, I was beginning to feel that I needed to expand my spiritual awareness to include the natural world. I wasn't sure exactly what that meant, or what a Nature-based spiritual system might look like for me, until I eventually discovered OBOD — The Order of Bards, Ovates & Druids — and began my spiritual journey by signing up for the Bardic Grade training course, which finally gave me the words to express the things I'd been feeling when I was out in Nature. It opened me up to a whole new way of connecting with the woods and the natural elements.

Finally, I want to mention the idea that Nature can be a mirror: a place that reflects back to us the things we need to see in ourselves. It can trigger the stuff that we need to bring to light so we can work on it in our personal development (things such as my lesson of *I am good enough*). It can also provide a space for deep healing. That's one of the many lessons that I received in this year of collecting tree stories, and as you'll soon see, their tales give us the opportunity to better connect with ourselves and get to know our true selves by connecting with Nature.

By now, you should have a pretty good idea of what this book is all about, and the journey you're about to join me on. To further clarify, this book is for you if:

- You love Nature and the outdoors
- You feel like there's something more to life, but you don't know what that is
- You're feeling disconnected from yourself, like your life has somehow gotten off track
- You feel like you don't really know who you are anymore...or maybe you've never truly known yourself at all
- Life is going just fine, but you have the suspicion that things could be much better
- You live your life in front of a computer screen or glued to your phone, and you're ready for something different

Throughout this book, you'll follow me on my journey as I connect on a deeper level with the trees, building relationships with them as the year goes by. You'll hear their stories, and you'll be given a series of experiments to carry out, should you choose to do so. These will help you to connect with yourself through connecting with Nature, and they'll open you up to the deep wisdom and healing that the trees can offer us. They will assist you in getting out of your head and into your body, so you can feel more deeply and truly experience all the joy that life has to offer. They'll add a new level of richness to your life that you may have never thought possible. I invite you to join me on my journey of collecting the trees' stories.

2

HOW TO USE THIS BOOK

How you use this book is entirely up to you, and you alone will know the best way for you to work through the chapters based on what's right for *you*. I'm not here to teach you anything; on the contrary, it's the trees who are the teachers in this book. I'm here to share my journey and my experience with the trees with you, and to facilitate your own personal growth by making the stories of the trees more readily available to you. *You're* the one who is actually going to do the work, should you choose to do so. Be sure to tailor this to fit your own personal wants and needs.

Now seems the appropriate time to share a confession with you: I'm not an expert in all this. Instead, I'm going down this path along with you. I may be one or more steps ahead of you on this journey, I may be walking alongside you, or I may even be walking behind you. We're all at different places on our path, moving along at our own pace.

Remember: in this book, as in life, only *you* know what's best for you. Take any advice you receive with a grain of salt, including the suggestions in this book. Take what serves you; leave what doesn't. Likewise, some of what's shared in this book will resonate with you, some of it may not. See what feels right to you and go from there. Some topics may require a stretch outside of your comfort zone; others may require you to expand your current belief system. *You do you.*

This book chronicles my experience throughout 2018 as I received and documented the stories of 28 trees. You can choose to read each chapter in order and experience the adventure and the stories as I did, in chronological order. If I were going to read this book, that's probably what I'd do, simply to get a feel for what the journey was like for the author.

You can also dip in and out as you like. You might want to open the book at a random point and read the chapter that you open up to. I've done that before with certain books, and I've often found that I "coincidentally" opened up the book to precisely the chapter that I needed to read at that time because it provided guidance or information on an issue or a topic that had been on my mind.

Or you could pick one species of tree and read through all the oak stories, then all the yew stories, then the sycamore stories. You might start with your favorite species of tree and then go from there. Or you might simply read through the table of contents and pick whichever chapter stands out to you or has a kind of zingy feeling to it.

One thing I need to mention: you may notice that the trees have a very peculiar way of telling their tales. There's a lot of repetition of words, phrases, and concepts. At times it almost feels like they're chanting a mantra. Again and again, as I was receiving the stories of the trees, I got the feeling that they think we humans need to hear something several times before it actually sinks in, and they're probably right. This means that you may find yourself reading and re-reading certain chapters and picking up on different details each time. I know that I have books that I've read and re-read and marked up with a different color pen each time, underlining different passages with each reading.

The trees' stories often include suggestions of activities for you to try: new ways of doing things, new actions to take, or new ways of looking at things. You might want to read the entire book first, and then go back and do some (or all) of the activities, or you might want to read each chapter and do the activity before moving onto the next chapter. Or, as I recommended earlier, you might open the book at random, then read the chapter and do the corresponding activity wherever you've opened up the book.

I do, however, urge you to give the activities a try: this is not a book that's simply meant to be read. It's meant to be *experienced*, and you can only get this experience by getting outdoors and taking the actions that are suggested by the trees. That means putting the book down at some point and going outside to meet the trees in your area — or taking the book outdoors with you to read it in the woods!

To make this easier, I've also created a full workbook based on this book, where you can not only work through the activities suggested by the trees, but you'll also have space to journal and write about your experiences. You can purchase that workbook wherever you bought this book, or visit my website to learn more.

Do not be bothered if you cannot find oaks, yews, and sycamores in your local region. You do not need to replicate my experiences, nor do you need to seek out the same species of trees. All trees have wisdom. All trees will help you to connect to the magical healing powers of Nature. Do what you can with what you have available to you in your local area. But I urge you: do not simply read. *Do. Be. Experience.* I wish you the best of luck on your journey!

For now, join me on my own adventure as I speak with the trees and receive their stories. They have great wisdom for you, and I can't wait for you to hear their tales. Let's get started.

PART II

1

LONE OAK

I was first drawn to this lone tree when I was walking through the woods by myself one afternoon. I had put together a route for the local walking group that I ran, and I was trying it out myself to see if I needed to make any adjustments before taking a group of people on the trail. This particular part of the route traversed a commercial forest, something that always made me feel a bit uncomfortable, as I mentioned in the Introduction. I had been walking in this area before — the woods between Coldharbour and Holmwood — and this part of the forest always felt off, as if something weren't quite right with the energy of the place. It felt devoid of wildlife, and it was missing the happy birdsong that I often heard in nearby native forests.

As I walked down the wide, smooth path, I looked all around on both sides of the trail, and I suddenly felt drawn to something on my right, as if my gaze were being held by a magnet located away from the trail and into the woods. And then I saw him: the lone tree. A majestic, ancient tree, his trunk gnarled and knotted. At first glance, he looked to be dead, but as I carefully made my way off the main trail and through the undergrowth, I could see small branches with green foliage on them, high up above. I gingerly picked my way towards him, zigzagging left and right, stepping over fallen branches from other trees, until I arrived at the base of the lone oak.

He was an imposing figure, standing out in a forest of evergreens. Old, wise. It was a miracle that he had been allowed to remain here on his own, amongst a sea of western hemlocks.

Oak is one of my favorite trees. I grew up in the hills across the bay from San Francisco, and it was not uncommon to see old oaks on my walks. When I traded the golden hills of California for the emerald hills of Surrey, I enjoyed seeing many large old oaks when I explored the local trails.

Oaks are one of the twenty trees of the Ogam, an early medieval alphabet that was used to write the early Irish language, though it has been argued that the earliest inscriptions in this alphabet may date back to the first century BCE. As I mentioned in Part I of this book, individual trees have been ascribed to each of the letters, and oak — or Duir, as it is called in Old Irish — is one of them.

Britain is home to two types of oaks — the pedunculate oak (*Quercus robur*) and the sessile oak (*Quercus petrea*). While many of the ancient oak forests that once blanketed the English countryside are now gone, having been cleared for agriculture and also for timber, many fine examples can be found throughout the country to this day. Oak has been long valued for its use in building ships and houses, and this has taken a toll on the ancient woodlands.

The English oak, or pedunculate oak, is a large deciduous tree that can reach up to 20-45 meters in height, with a girth of up to 14 meters. As these oaks mature, they form a broad, spreading crown which is supported by sturdy branches underneath the canopy. Because their crown is light and open, it enables sunlight to penetrate through to the forest floor, which encourages the growth of wildflowers underneath. As young trees, they're fast growers and only begin to slow down once they reach about 120 years old.

The mature oak is an imposing figure that stands out in a forest, or when a lone oak is found on a grassy hillside. It's not surprising that the tree has come to symbolize strength and endurance, generosity and protection, justice and honesty. It is said to be a doorway to the mysteries of this world, a boundary crossing between one place and the next. It symbolizes inner knowledge, and the ability to see the invisible.

Oak is said to hold the magical properties of protecting a person against colds in the winter if a falling oak leaf is caught. Burning an oak wood fire in the hearth is said to cure illness, and carrying an acorn is thought to protect against pain and illness. Carrying any piece of oak — assuming that it was taken with permission and that gratitude was given to the tree — is said to attract good luck to the holder.

It was clear from the moment we met that this lone oak had a story to tell and that he wanted to be heard. But it was cold, and I didn't relish the idea of sitting still to receive his tale in the middle of winter. And so, two months later, on the spring equinox, I made my way back to him to hear his tale. It was a sunny day, and the clear blue sky was filled with puffy white clouds. There was a crisp feeling to the air. It had snowed the day before, and tiny pockets of white were still visible throughout the shady forest.

I picked my way through the wood until I reached the

base of his trunk. I pulled off my backpack, setting it on the ground near the oak, and I put on my hat, gloves, and neck warmer before sitting down next to him. My body was still warm from the walk, but I knew I would soon feel a chill as I settled in to receive his story, and I wanted to prepare for this in advance. I touched his trunk with both hands and rested my forehead against his trunk. It was not quite a hug; it was my customary ritual for greeting trees at this time.

He spoke:

Once upon a time, this was a natural forest, a native forest. A forest of mixed evergreens and deciduous trees, and we all lived in peace and quiet and silence. It was a kind of natural harmony.

There were local people here in this area, people who would occasionally walk through this forest, down the trails that you see today. And sometimes one would stop and have a meal underneath my boughs. They would rest up against my trunk, and then they would move on. This was a peaceful wood.

It is no longer so: now you hear the roar of the chainsaw off in the distance. That sound came to us, and my friends — my family — were cut down to make way for an evergreen forest. Not a forest really, but a plantation. A plantation of trees, a colony of trees, made up of just one kind of tree.

For some reason they let me stay. They cut down the trees all around me — my network, my family — and planted these evergreens, the ancestors of those which you see today. The diversity of our community was gone.

I do not begrudge my new neighbors — it was not their fault. It was not their hand that cut the native forest. And they are beautiful, as all trees are: green all year round, lush undergrowth, tiny trees at the base, and straight, naked, trunks. It is a pleasant view. Although I miss my friends from long ago, I understand that your culture may need these trees, may need these products, and may need this work to be carried out.

It feels unnatural, though. They grow so straight that it saddens me because this is not a forest. It is simply a field of trees, a hillside of trees. You may hear a pheasant off in the distance, smaller birds chirping up high. There is life here, but not like there used to be.

People often say that if the trees could talk, what stories they'd tell. And we have stories, we do have stories....

Humans want things to happen quickly, but in the world of the trees, life is slow, life is long, at least for those of us who are natural trees, native trees. The ones who have been planted here will be harvested, just like another crop, as if they were a field of wheat, or oats, or rye. They will be gone, and the field will be empty until new trees are planted. It is slow, and it is long, and it is a peaceful process...until harvest time comes again. And every time they come to cut the trees, I fear that I will be included, that I will be seen as a nuisance, or that I will be struck by one of the falling trees and damaged, and so they decide to take me out, too.

Life isn't what it was back then, back when this was a native forest.

I am aware that perhaps this was not the story that you wanted to hear. Perhaps you wanted something quaint, and pretty; something heart-warming, something funny. Other trees will have those stories for you, not I. For I cannot forget my friends, my family, and my network. I cannot deny the fact that I am one of a kind here in this field of trees. Up here on the hill-side; alone, yet not alone. Surrounded by trees that are not like me.

You may not want to include my story in your book at all; you may not want to put it at the beginning, as one of the first stories, even though I am the first tree that you are talking to.

Mine is not a light-hearted tale. And yet this story needs to be told.

People know about commercial forests, as they call them, people know about these fields of trees, not native; and yet, they have not heard the story from the tree's perspective. People walk down these paths and they say: "How beautiful, an evergreen forest", and they might even see me as they look off to the side, down the path, and notice that I am different. They might be surprised that I am one of a kind, but most do not look. Most of the people who walk through this field of trees in these times, they keep their eyes on the path, chatting amongst themselves, having their own conversations, deeply engaged with each other and not really connecting with the world around them, with the path, with what lies on both sides of the path; with the trees, the birds — birds are simply background noise to them, a pretty song. Or they might not even hear the birds, so engrossed they may be in their conversations.

But if they were to stop, and sit on a fallen log or with their back up against a tree and close their eyes, they could hear the life that is in the woods: the little birds chirping, the pheasants getting startled by something... the slight hum of the cars off in the distance. There are no roads through here, but we can hear your vehicles. It is like a hum that never ends. Your airplanes flying above, mingled with the pheasants calling out to each other, the rustling of the leaves, the fronds of the evergreens as the wind blows a little bit.

They might open their eyes and see the blue sky and the white clouds, just barely visible in between the branches of the evergreens up above. But to see all these things, and to hear all these things, it is necessary to stop, to sit, to be still, to experience the woods, to experience this field of trees, as I call it. For there is so much here — so much going on. If only you would stop and sit and allow your ears to open up to the sounds, and your eyes to look all around you, and take in what appears to be a very still, very quiet place.

This is experiencing the woods; this is experiencing the forest. And yet most people simply walk on by, walk down the trail, walk down the path. This trail is simply a means to get to their destination, and yet the journey in itself has so much. It has so much to offer.

And so, I would like to suggest to those who hear my story: the next time they find themselves out in the woods, or even in a park — the next time they find themselves outdoors in Nature — to sit, to be still, to take in the sounds, both human-made and Nature-made. The roar of an airplane overhead can feel so jarring, but it is part of this world that we are in today, a world that did not exist when I first came to be. But it is the world we are in right now.

Trees. Birds. Leaves.

Sit, and be still, and pay attention. Open your ears, open your eyes; this is experiencing Nature with all your senses; reach out and touch a leaf, a branch...the ground, the soil...the earth...the bark of a tree. We love being touched. We love it when people make contact with us. We like to engage; we like to interact. We must wait for you to come to us. And it so rarely happens. We should be used to it by now, but still, it surprises us. In the same way that two humans would like a hug — or a dog, or a cat, would like to be stroked — we too like contact, touch. Feel the texture of our bark and say hello as you walk by. Not to every tree in the forest, we don't expect that. But we are all individuals just as you are, we all have personalities, although you cannot usually tell this if you are just walking quickly through the woods. We each have a life. We are each a living being, though we do not have a face, though we do not talk with voices out loud as you do. We are all individuals, just as you are. And we long for connection — interaction — not just among ourselves, but with people.

If you were to speak with each of the trees in this tree-field, or in a forest, in a wood, you would get different stories, you would get different voices. You would get different personalities. People look at a forest, especially a commercial forest, like this — a tree-field — and they think that they are all the same, that we are all the same. I am different, of course, to the human eye but my neighbors look like copies of the same tree, though they are each living individuals. Each with a voice, each with a story, these — my neighbors — are young, unlike me. But they have stories, they have voices, and they are each as unique as each of you humans, although they may look similar, although they may even look the same to you.

This is what I wish to share with you. There is diversity in sameness. Even if we look the same, we are different. Some trees would look at humans and say they all look the same, but you know that you do not. You are not the same; you are different, just as we are.

You are cold. It is time for you to go; you can always come back for more....

~

THE LONE OAK's words were as much for me personally as they were for this book. I have the tendency to always be in motion: each year for the past two years I've done the Walk 1,000 Miles Challenge. This encourages me to get outdoors, to spend time in Nature, and to get more exercise. Each year, it has pushed me a little bit and it has given me the motivation to go outside even on days when I didn't really feel like it.

While I enjoy the challenge, and while it has served its purpose for me, it's also kept me walking, walking, walking. I'm always on the move when I'm out in Nature: I've got to get those extra miles in. It makes me less likely to stop and linger in the woods, which is a shame. And while I am, of course, walking with my eyes open, I often see only the bigger picture of the landscape I'm passing through, while ignoring the details of the forest. It's as though I'm looking without actually seeing; hearing without truly listening.

It's very fitting that this was the first message that I received from the trees: this year was all about walking, though it was also about me sitting still to receive tree stories. For the first time, I slowed down more and stopped to listen: not just to the trees and to their tales, but also to all the little sounds that are a part of a living forest. There's always so much going on, both human-made and Nature-made, as the Lone Oak put it.

You may be wondering how the Lone Oak knew that he was the first tree I visited to collect a story. I believe that when I open up to channel, a connection is formed that allows information to flow between the two of us, and the spirit of the tree has access to the same information that I have access to. I also believe that tree spirits are connected to all that is, which means that they can easily tap into that information. We, too, are connected to everything in the universe, but often our own limiting beliefs can get in the way of accessing all the information that is available to us.

As I progressed throughout my journey this year to collect the stories of trees, it was also interesting for me to get a feel for the different species of trees. My favorites have always been oaks, yews, and hollies, but this year opened me to up connect more with other types of trees, including sycamores, beeches, and western hemlocks. In fact, I wasn't even sure the Lone Oak was actually an oak. I ended up sending an email to the Forestry Commission to ask about the Lone Oak because I wasn't completely sure what it was. It looked kind of like an old oak, but the bark wasn't quite right.

It wasn't long before I received a reply from forester Nick: he was "a dead pedunculate oak (*Quercus robur*). The deformations on its stem are known as burs. You may have got the foliage confused with the surrounding evergreen trees, which appear to mainly be Western Hemlock."

I was confused: I had a conversation with this tree; how could it be dead? And I definitely did see foliage up at the top; it wasn't branches from the surrounding hemlocks. But upon further visits to the Lone Oak, I could see that the forester was correct: it seemed as though the surrounding hemlocks had spread their seeds, and some had come to rest in the upper boughs of the old oak.

This explained the greenery, but it didn't explain the conversation we had. After some reflection, I remembered the concept of the "wood wide web" — the mycorrhizal network of fungi that connects individual plants and trees and transfers water, nutrients, minerals, and information between them. Perhaps the spirit of the Lone Oak lingered in the network? That was the best explanation I could come up with. It seemed that the tree's body was dead — or appeared to be — but its spirit stayed on. Perhaps the hemlock seedlings provided a kind of link to the network.

~

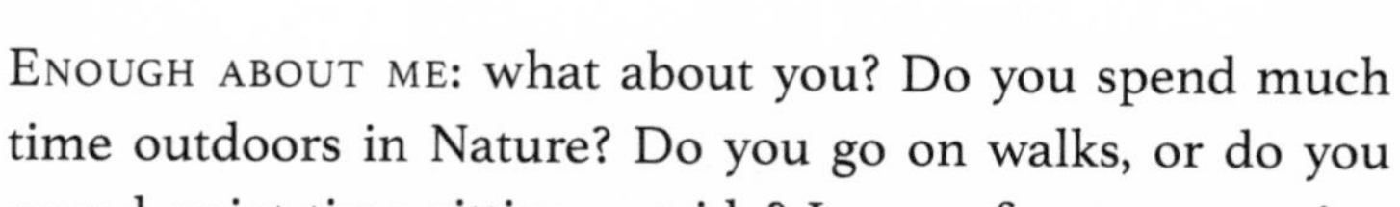

Enough about me: what about you? Do you spend much time outdoors in Nature? Do you go on walks, or do you spend quiet time sitting outside? Is your focus on moving through Nature, or being still in Nature? Do you ever stop and take the time to really observe all the sounds of the outdoors? If you were to plan an excursion somewhere that you could sit in stillness in Nature, where would you go? To a park or to a woodland? Or somewhere else, like a river-bank, a lake, or an ocean?

And what about the trees themselves? Can you identify the different species of trees in your area? Would you like to be able to do this, maybe by purchasing a guidebook to trees in your area? Do you ever stop to notice the differences between the individual trees of each species and compare two oaks or two yews, for example?

2

CHALICE WELL YEWS

Glastonbury, home of the fabled Isle of Avalon, is also home to two sacred springs: the White Spring and the Red Spring, both of which are located at the foot of the Glastonbury Tor, the large conical hill that rises up above the town and is visible from all around. The Red Spring is located within the grounds of the Chalice Well Trust Gardens. Surrounded by beautiful gardens and an apple orchard, it is a peaceful haven where visitors can experience the tranquility of this sacred site. For over two thousand years this has been a place of pilgrimage where people have come to drink and to bathe in the water of the spring. It's one of my favorite places to visit in Glastonbury, and it's a place where I've spent long hours in silence: reading, wandering, gazing at the abundance of flowers and foliage, and sitting on the stone benches that surround the sacred well itself.

I am a Companion of the Chalice Well Trust Gardens, which means that for a small annual membership fee, I gain free admission to the gardens all year round and I can also book a room in the Little St. Michael's retreat house which is located near the entrance. For Easter weekend, I booked a three-night stay at the retreat house, which allows 24-hour access to the garden, an unusual treat that I had never before experienced. On the first night of my stay, it was chilly and dark and drizzly, and I gingerly stepped out from the warmth of the retreat house and into the garden. I was determined to take advantage of the privilege of visiting the garden at nighttime.

It felt strange to be alone — at least, I presumed I was alone — in the garden. It was so cold and wet that I didn't think anyone else was out, but it was so dark that I couldn't be sure. There was no lighting, and all I had was a small flashlight to help me find my way. I couldn't see much beyond a few feet all around me; the rest was total darkness.

I had been to the garden many times during the day, but never at nighttime, and as I carefully navigated the wet paths that snaked through the garden, I found myself gravitating to the two giant yew trees that sit above the Vesica Pool and form a sort of informal gateway into the depths of the garden beyond. I usually began each visit to the garden by passing between these two yews.

Yew trees (*Taxus baccata*) are a very long-lived evergreen conifer that is native to Britain, Europe, and North Africa. Mature yews can grow to 20 meters in height, and have a gorgeous reddish-brown bark, which is flaky and often peels to reveal darker burgundy or almost purple tones underneath. The bark of wet yews can sometimes look as though the trees are bleeding. Small, almost insignificant flowers bloom in March and April, with red, fleshy fruits called arils to follow. All parts of the yew except for the aril are toxic, though the seed inside the aril is also toxic.

The yew is one of most long-lived trees in northern Europe, with lifespans of up to 4,000 years old (though some believe the St Cynog yew in Wales is 5,000 years old), and the most ancient individuals — one of whom you'll meet in Chapter 5 — have gorgeous, gnarled trunks, which sometimes split into two, leaving a hollow in the middle of the tree.

If you undertake a study of some of the most ancient yews of Britain, you'll notice that many of them are located in churchyards, yet the trees clearly outdate the churches themselves. The yew was revered by the ancient druids (and also by modern druids) who often used yew groves for their sacred ceremonies. When Christianity came to Britain, many of these sacred groves were appropriated by the new religion, and churches were built alongside the yews.

The yew — or Ioho, as it is known in Old Irish — is another of the twenty trees of the Ogam. The yew tree has come to symbolize immortality, rebirth, longevity, and strength, and is thought to have these same magical properties for those who work with it. The yew represents transformation, change in life direction, and change in general. It reminds us that there are other levels of existence beyond those that we can see with the naked eye, and it provides access to the spirit realms. Yews are not only incredibly long-lived trees, but they also have the capacity to regenerate themselves: often new growth will appear in a hollow trunk, and when a yew is given enough space and freedom to grow as it pleases, its drooping branches may re-root when they touch the earth. Yew was traditionally used in the construction of long bows, and it is now a popular wood for making magical tools such as wands and dowsing rods. It is a strong wood that resists decay.

These yews of the Chalice Well Gardens were old and well established, but not old enough to have split trunks, and were standing straight and tall. I walked up to the nearest one and placed my hands on its trunk to make contact. I was so pleased to be able to connect with the trees at nighttime, as they were located in a very exposed location of the garden where I wouldn't normally feel comfortable communicating with them during daylight hours when the garden was full of visitors. He immediately began his story:

WE ARE NOT SO old as to remember the days when the people still worshipped the gods and the goddesses; when this land really was a sacred place and was seen by all as a place of pilgrimage. But we have heard the stories. We have heard the stories from our ancestors because, you see, we trees have a network: a network that interconnects all of us in a region. And in the same way that you humans pass stories down from grandparents, to children, to grandchildren, to great-grandchildren, we too pass our stories down, from generation to generation of trees. And this is how you will have access to some of the older stories that we have.

These are stories that are stored in the network of all of us trees. The network is there — available — for each of us to pick up, to learn from, to treasure; and to keep the stories alive in the network, to pass them on to future generations.

I am a yew. I am an old yew, but not as old as we can get. You may have seen ancient, ancient yews; hundreds and hundreds of years old. More than a thousand, more than 1,500 years old — we are long-lived trees. And so, our memories in the network can reach far back — and we have much to contribute in keeping these stories alive across generations.

This land that you are on has always been considered sacred. People come here now, and all they see are pretty gardens: a place to come as tourists. They might feel a sense of relaxation here, but it is not until they sit, still and quiet, on a bench by the water, or with their back up against one of our trees, that they can slip into that deep, deep state of relaxation. The worries and the stress of their day-to-day lives slip away, and they are able to sense — a deep sense — of just how special this place is. It is the relaxation that is the sign for them because it is perhaps a sensation that they have not felt before, or that they rarely feel. And this is the sign to them that this is a sacred place, that this is a special place.

But, as I said, not everyone feels this, not everyone senses this. In fact, few people do.

The tourists, the people who are rushing through, completing a quick circuit of the gardens, on their way onto their next tourist stop, perhaps to go shopping in town on the High Street... they will not sense this. They might even be confused as to why it was recommended that they come here: at first glance, it is just a garden, a small ten-acre garden, well taken care of, well-loved by the people who do know just how special this land is. But even those who do not sense the energy here, or the spirits of this land, or the sacredness, they will still take away a seed, a small seed of this sacredness, a small seed of this experience: a small seed that may germinate in the future, or it may sit dormant in their soul, in their minds, in their being, for years... years... years. Until it may germinate, or not.

It is not necessary that everyone recognize the specialness of this place. What is important is that they come here, even as fast-paced tourists, because they will carry that seed. And perhaps they will recommend it to others...and perhaps they will not. But the more people who come here, the more people will experience this and take away a bit of this energy with them, wherever they go, when they return to their normal lives.

A bit of magic — like fairy dust, you might call it. There is no actual dust, of course: it is that sparkle of an energy of the sacredness of this land, of the water, of the spring, of the twin springs. You sense this. Many do.

And when you come to places where you sense this special energy, this special feeling of relaxation, this special feeling of goodness, we would recommend that you sit still, and you bathe in the energy. You can meditate if you know how to do so. Or simply sit, eyes opened, eyes closed, whatever works for you. And we would recommend that you take in — that you bathe in — the magic of this place or of places like this. Once you have felt that feeling, you will be able to recognize it in other places, even other places which you may not know to be sacred, which you may not know to be special, but you will recognize this feeling — it is like a kindred sensation.

We know that the other tree has told you to sit and be still. You may feel frustrated that you are hearing a similar suggestion here. This may be a message that you hear often from us trees because as you know this is something that we are very good at; we are not mobile like you humans.

We sit. We stand. And we are still.

Not completely still, of course: our branches move with the wind, our leaves, our fronds...our needles, if we are a pine. There is movement. But we are firmly rooted in one spot, allowing us to bathe in the deep energy of each place, of the place where we are. And so, we are like a sponge: a sponge for this energy. We can absorb it, and we can radiate it out. This is why some people are drawn to trees, especially to trees in these sacred places.

And the two of us here are like twins; we are like a doorway to this special world. A doorway to this sacred place of water, to the sacred spring, the Red Spring... flowing... flowing... you can hear it all the time in the background. You can hear it bubbling to the left, you can hear it bubbling to the right.

And we are very grateful to have been planted here in this garden. This is one of the most beautiful places we could be.

Sacred, sacred, sacred spring. Sacred, sacred, water. Sacred energy.

We are happy to be here, and we are happy to welcome: to welcome visitors as we do, standing as sentries in the entrance that leads up to the first bathing pool... and the waterfall beyond... and the fountain beyond that... and the well beyond that. We are a gateway to all the goodness that lies in this garden.

We are happy to be here and we are happy to welcome, always happy to welcome. This is all.

THERE IS MORE. (I returned to the yews on the second night of my stay, this time approaching the second of the two.)

You sometimes see people placing their hands and their head against my bark — just as you do when you make first contact. Sometimes they do it because they expect to feel something. Or they think that is how they should make contact. It is certainly one way to create a connection with us, this is true. It is an attempt, and we welcome all attempts to connect with us. We welcome human touch when it is kind, when it is gentle, when it is friendly, when it is peaceful... a hand against our bark, a gentle brushing of our leaves.

We welcome these things. We welcome this contact because we know this means that we are more than just scenery to you — part of the landscape — that perhaps you see us as the living beings that we are. Perhaps you do not understand that we are so unique as individuals. Perhaps you do not understand the respect that we deserve, that our lives deserve.

But it helps the connection; it helps to strengthen the connection. It helps open the communication: even if you do not understand what you are receiving, what you are sending, what you are transmitting. We welcome this touch: it is a start. It is a start. All is good.

There is not much we can say to you right now, and yet there is so much we can say to you. But the message that we have for you, the two of us — the two yews — is this: contact. We relish contact, we invite contact.

Go. Speak to my partner. (I returned to the first yew; the one I had spoken with on the previous night).

Welcome. I was feeling a bit neglected. (I laughed at this).

As my partner said: we are different, each of us. He and I are different — and each of us is different from all the other yews, all the other trees, all the other plants.

And so... we invite you to get to know each tree as an individual. Start with a certain type of tree, such as us, the yews.

Touch our bark. Smell our bark. Make contact. Sit with your back against our trunks. Walk around each of us in a circle. And repeat with other yews, to sense how different we all are... our shape, our form, our texture, our height, our girth. These are things that are easy for you to see, easy for you to feel, easy for you to sense. Sense our energy, sense how our energy is different. When you have done this, step back and think: that in the same way that we are different physically, we are different energetically, and we are different inside. That our being is different means that our soul is different. We are each different individuals.

We invite you: get to know the yews, get to know the elders, get to know the oaks, get to know the hollies — they are prickly, but you can approach them. Get to know each of the different kinds of trees, but get to know multiple individual trees within each one, within each type of tree. Really sense the difference: the difference between each of you, between each of us... that we are individuals, that sense that we are individuals.

Know this. Feel this. Sense this.

You can see, for example, that I am different from my

partner — I am wider than my partner, I am a bigger tree and I have a different form. And yet, we were planted at the same time, we as a pair, we as partners guarding the entrance to this place, one of the entrances to this place.

We welcome you to sense us, to feel us, to connect with us, to communicate with us. And to those of you who think that you cannot communicate with us — we invite you to see, hear, feel. For these things you can do, these things you know how to do. These things you absolutely can experience, even if you think that you cannot talk to trees; or that you can talk to trees but cannot hear our answers. Communication comes in so many forms, so many forms. And we invite you: see us...hear us...feel us...touch us...smell us. Use your senses to connect with us.

This is communication. Not all communication must be verbal. Not all communication must be verbal, I repeat this. You humans rely very much on verbal connection, on verbal communication; but there are other types of communication that are even more subtle... that are just as valid, that are just as satisfying, that are just as connective.

And we invite you.

Now return to my partner, for he has parting words. (I returned to the other yew).

Hello again. I could echo all that my partner said, for it is all important. We invite you to start with a tree that has always caught your attention, or with the next tree that you see. We invite you to go out into a park, a wood, anywhere that you can easily connect with a tree; where you can easily see a tree; where you can easily spend just a few minutes alone with a tree.

We understand that you may feel self-conscious: you may think that people will stare at you. Find a quiet place to connect with this tree. A place where perhaps you may not be seen, and allow yourself... allow yourself to connect.

Connect without expectations. Connect with an open mind; connect with an open heart. Connect, connect, connect.

This is all we ask, that you take the first step, just one step and that first step is to connect. To see. To hear. To feel.

That is all.

THE MESSAGE from the Chalice Well Yews came in two parts, on two subsequent nights. The first night, I was honestly a bit creeped out because I was so focused on the tree's message that I became totally detached from my awareness of my surroundings. It made me feel vulnerable in the dark garden. At one point, I was certain that I felt a touch on my right shoulder, which sent my stomach leaping and tore my awareness from the tree. It wasn't long after that when I decided that perhaps it was time to head back into the retreat house and up to my room for the night, even though I knew there was more for me to receive.

I braved the dark, cold, and damp weather a second time the following night to get the next part of the message. Again, I felt slightly uncomfortable with being alone in the dark as I was essentially unaware of my surroundings when I fully tuned into the trees' message. A part of me knew that I was not alone and that there were unseen beings around me — Nature spirits, perhaps — and I was always a bit uncomfortable when I sensed things were there that I could not see.

We, humans, place a great deal of importance on the things that we *see*, and I myself am a particularly visual person. I learn best through seeing and reading, and when I channel, I often do it by writing. This journey of collecting tree stories was helping me to learn and to receive messages in a different way, by verbally channeling. Perhaps I could have chronicled their messages by directly writing them down, but they seemed to flow so quickly and smoothly that it was easiest to just speak them out loud into a recorder.

That's why it made me so uncomfortable to sense the presence of unseen beings or Nature spirits. I know they're there, but because I can't *see* them, a sense of fear creeps into my body. I know I'm safe; I know they're friendly. I can sense that much. But the fact that I can't *see* them, only sense their energy, is unnerving.

In the same way that I can sense the energy of unseen beings, I can also sense the energy of sacred sites. Over and over again, I've been drawn to visit some of the better-known sites like Glastonbury and Avebury, and also some of the lesser known places such as West Kennet Long Barrow in Wiltshire and Mag's Well in the Surrey Hills. But it wasn't until I heard the message from this pair of yews that I understood the importance of simply bathing in this energy. Sometimes we don't actually need to *do* anything at all; we simply need to *be* in this energy.

Glastonbury is considered by many to be a sacred site. It's been associated with many ancient legends: it's supposedly the final resting place of King Arthur and it is said to have been visited by Joseph of Arimathea and Jesus. It is also supposed to be the burial place of the Holy Grail: the Holy Chalice which was used by Christ at the Last Supper. Not just the locale of many Christian and secular legends, Glastonbury is also considered to be a sacred site by many pagan traditions. OBOD, the Druid order that I belong to, meets there twice a year, in summer and in winter.

I loved that the yews saw themselves — and other trees — as librarians of the forest, keeping the tales of the woodlands alive generation after generation, passing the stories down through their network. It gave me a sense of both the magnitude and the ancientness of their community, and it increased my sense of the importance of sharing these tales with the world.

Sometimes we need to hear a message or receive a lesson over and over again so that it finally sinks in. That's why it was no surprise to me that the Chalice Well Yews echoed the lesson of the Lone Oak to be still in Nature — and this wouldn't be the last time I heard this advice from the trees.

From the very first time I spoke to a tree (and listened to its response), I began to place my hands on a tree's trunk to make my first contact. Throughout my year of collecting tree stories, I began to do this more and more: I began to *feel* the trees, to *touch* the trees. Making physical contact with them helped me to connect with the trees on another level, and it felt as though it deepened the relationship with them.

WHAT ABOUT YOU? Have you ever visited a place where you felt a very special kind of energy? Do you know of any places out in Nature that have a sacred feel to them? Have you ever visited them with the intention of just bathing in the energy, or do you feel like you have to do something special while you're there? Is this something you'd like to try? If so, where would you go?

Have you ever felt like you weren't alone when you were out in Nature, and yet couldn't see anyone else around? How does this make you feel? Are you curious, or frightened? If you feel uncomfortable when this occurs, what might make you feel more at ease?

How often do you actually make physical contact with the trees you pass on your walks, whether it's in a park, in a garden, or in a forest? Do you ever touch them? Do you reach out to feel their bark, their leaves, or their fruits? How do you feel about making more physical contact with the trees you see?

And what about seeing the different trees as individuals? This is the second time we've heard this suggestion — to feel into the differences between individual trees. What is this like for you? Can you really differentiate between the trees in a woodland, or do they all look the same to you?

3

JUNIPER BOTTOM YEWS

After I did my Lowland Leader training in April, a course designed to help me guide my monthly walking groups through lowland areas, I decided to spend more time exploring Box Hill, which is located very near to where I live. I had been told that the assessment for the course was usually held in this area, and I wanted to explore some of the parts of the hill that I wasn't as familiar with. Box Hill is mostly made up of open access land, which means that — thanks to the Countryside and Rights of Way Act of 2000 — the public has the right to roam freely throughout the land, rather than being restricted to the signposted public footpaths and bridleways. Narrow trails and cycle paths wind their way through the native woodland, making it the perfect place to explore. The western part of Box Hill, where most of the trails are located, is owned by the National Trust, which is an independent charity and membership organization for environmental and heritage conservation in England, Wales, and Northern Ireland.

Box Hill is named for the ancient box woodland which is found on the western-facing slope of the hill. Boxwood, or *Buxus sempervirens*, is an evergreen shrub or small tree that you might be most familiar with in the form of ornamental hedging or topiaries in formal gardens. Box, however, is not the subject of this chapter. In addition to the extensive box woodland found on Box Hill, there are also a number of large, ancient yew trees.

I found myself walking deeper and deeper into the forest, winding back and forth through deep woodland on a very narrow switchback trail that was clearly designed for cycles rather than walkers, and this soon grew rather tedious. The trail eventually came out of the woods onto a public footpath that bordered the woodland, where I turned right, soon turning right again onto a bridleway that ran through the bottom of Happy Valley and up a slight incline. This was an open trail, with views to either side, that rose in elevation ever so slightly as I walked along it. It was flanked by two slopes on both sides, and the path itself was very exposed to the elements, which on this day was the hot sunshine. Despite the fact that Box Hill is usually a very popular walking destination on the weekends, this was a weekday and it had been over an hour since I crossed paths with another person.

The day was very hot and sunny, and I found myself feeling a bit tired of the heat as I walked along the open trail. I had my sun hat on, and my face and arms were slathered with sun cream, but the heat was just a bit much for my liking. It was the first truly hot day of what would turn out to be scorching summer, and I wasn't used to this kind of weather. The ice cubes that I had added to keep my water pouch cool had long melted, thanks to the heat of the sun and the warmth of my back. As I passed a small grove of yew trees to the right of the trail, I felt a calling. Ignoring it, I continued walking straight down the path. I was hot and tired, and I wanted shade, which I knew lay ahead of me, up the hill.

Realizing what I had done — I had ignored the call of a tree — I stopped, turned around, and backtracked down the trail. I walked up into the little grove, approached one of the yews, and settled down in its shade, resting my back against its trunk. The tree was cool, and the little grove offered a welcome respite from the sun and the heat of the trail. Immediately, the yew began to speak.

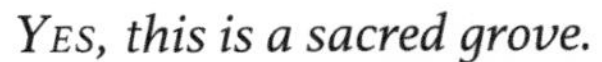

Yes, this is a sacred grove.

You felt drawn to our energy as you were walking down the trail, and you saw the little path leading into the clearing in the center of the trees. You sensed that there was a reason you had to step off the trail, not necessarily because you wanted to take a break, but because there was something special here. And yet, you hesitated. You hesitated because this was not on your intended path, and this is a message that I have for you right now: sometimes you are on a path walking through the woods, a literal path, or it could be the path of your life that you are on at any given time.

So, sometimes you are on a path, you have a plan, you are walking down the path, you are trying to get from one place to the other, walking, walking, walking and your eye is caught by something just off the path. It could be off to your right, off to your left, and so you walk off this path...or you do not. You might stand there for a moment hesitating, confused, reluctant: reluctant to step off your path, to step off that well-beaten path, to step off the path that you had planned, the planned path that you were traveling on. You may like plans. You may not like to deviate from the path, but sometimes it is necessary: sometimes it is beneficial, sometimes it can help you see things, experience things that you had not planned, things that are a surprise to you, things that you did not expect.

Like a small clearing in the trees.

It could be something as simple as the small clearing in the trees, a place where you sit with your back up against one of them, one of the cool trees on this hot day. And the coolness of the tree — the smoothness of its bark — is restful, it cools you down, it allows you to relax and recharge and then continue on your path. Or... it could be something else. It could be a discovery of something new. A discovery of something different, a discovery of a new trail, a new path that leads to something unknown, a sense of adventure.

And this is why we are the trees of a grove. This is why we would encourage you to step off the trail that you have planned, step off the path that you have planned, and meander, discover, walk, wander...without knowing where you are going, and see where the path leads you. Pay attention to your gut, to your intuition, to the places to which you are drawn when you are walking along your path: you must be aware. It can be easy to just blindly follow a trail, a path, without really paying attention to what's going on — on either side of the trail.

But when you are aware, when you are walking with your eyes open, with your ears open, with your senses alert, that is when you can easily see the little places where you might veer off the path and discover something new, discover something worthwhile, discover something different — and then allow that sense of adventure to be ignited in your life. So many people live routine, daily lives, with no sense of adventure, no sense of fun, with no sense of joy, with no sense of excitement about what may come: so much routine, so much routine. And yet, it can be so easy to allow the adventure into your life in the same way that if you practice as you walk through the woods, you practice being alert, you practice being aware, and you allow yourself... you give yourself permission to be drawn down these side paths and side trails.

Once you re-train yourself to allow these side trips to happen, then it will be easier for you to do the same in your life and to veer off the plan that you have had for yourself, the path that you are walking, the metaphorical path. It will be easier for you to veer from that path when you see something that catches your eye — something that might give you that sense of adventure, that unexpected adventure of new paths, of new things, and it will be easier for you to follow these intuitive nudges off the main road.

This grove has been here for years and years and years.

Now that you are sitting here with your back up against one of us, you can see the other yews: two straight in front of you, three off to your left and another big one up the hill. We have been here so long, just to the right of the path. And yet so few people come to visit us. So few people come to sit with their back against one of our trunks and to rest in the shade that we offer. So many people walk by without even noticing us, without even seeing us, because they are lost in conversation, not paying attention to the riches, to the sensations, which lie on both sides of the path: the visual riches, the sensual riches. The smell of the trees, of the earth and the flowers — many people miss these things.

And we are aware that other trees have given you this story: this slowing down, of stopping, of resting, of sitting, of listening, of seeing, of hearing, of enjoying, of taking in through your senses all that is around you. And yet, it is something that we can all recommend because we are trees.

We stand here for years and years and years watching the people go by, the birds, the animals... and we stand.

It is precisely because of this immobility of ours that we would recommend that you stray from your path: you do not see all the options that you have available to you — most people do not. Most people miss this tiny little trail, that tiny little trail, that little path that comes off the main path and leads to our grove here. And if you open your eyes, and you open your senses, and you become aware of these little things, it can be life-changing for you: you who are able to walk, you who are able to be mobile, you who are able to walk both physically and metaphorically down a path through your life, experiencing things. This is all about the experience. It is all about the adventure of new experiences, of unexpected experiences.

This is what you crave when it has been a long time since the last time you have done a long-distance trail: it is that adventure of walking somewhere new, of seeing someplace new, of walking and walking and walking and not knowing what exactly is to come. You may have a map, you may have a guidebook with indications of what you will see along the path, but it is the adventure of actually experiencing those things.

And that is why we encourage you to stray from the path so that you can experience that sense of adventure. Take the detour. Take the little trail. And again, we mean this not just literally, but metaphorically.

Be aware — with all your senses. Pay attention to the things that catch you up, and be open to exploring. Be open to giving yourself permission to take the detour.

This is all.

THIS YEW KNEW EXACTLY how difficult it was for me to stray off the beaten path. I'm very guilty of simply keeping my eyes on the trail ahead and walking, walking, walking my thousand miles so I can achieve my goal each year. I'm very good at keeping my eye on the target, and not so good at taking in the entire panoramic view. It's often only when I climb to the top of a hill that I allow myself to stop and enjoy the view all around me.

This is true both literally when I'm walking out in Nature, and also figuratively when I'm working on achieving my goals in life. I create a system for tracking my progress toward my goals, and I do, do, do until I achieve them. In fact, good friends know very well my fondness for spreadsheets and tracking: so much so, that I was once asked to record an episode for my Into the Woods podcast (which explores themes of mindset, personal development, and connection with Nature) on exactly how I manage to achieve my goals and do all the things I set out to do each year.

When I first moved to the Surrey Hills, I spent hours and hours out in Nature, exploring all the public footpaths and bridleways and open access land that were so abundant in the area. I would often set out with no particular destination in mind, other than the goal of exploring new paths. Eventually, I covered most of the surrounding area, and there were no more surprises. At that point, I began using online maps to seek out new trails that I was unfamiliar with and charting specific walking routes that would take me down those paths. This allowed me to see new territory, but it lacked the spontaneity of simply turning off down a path I had never seen before, which I had loved.

The Juniper Bottom Yew was right: I enjoyed the sense of adventure I got whenever I walked a long-distance trail such as a National Trail. I relished that feeling of stepping out into the unknown and walking thirty, seventy, one hundred miles to my destination. Walking a long-distance trail takes me out of my known territory and into new places, which was always exciting. But I was also aware that I had the tendency to stick to the path and not veer off to the myriad of attractions that were often found just a mile or two off the main trail.

I had learned early on, when I walked the South Downs Way — my first long-distance trail — that detours only added to my daily mileage and often made an already challenging experience even more difficult and painful. This had led me to be overly cautious, avoiding local attractions that were off the main trail, and then returning to them at a later date if I really wanted to visit them. This made the journey a bit easier, but it also took some of the adventure and spontaneity out of the whole experience. It almost made things a little bit too serious.

I resolved to listen to the yew's advice and be more flexible on my next long-distance walk...and, perhaps most importantly: to pay attention to the signs and to notice when it was necessary to stray off the planned route. I also resolved to remember that even when I am walking one of the same footpaths that I've walked down over and over again, it is never the same. The seasons change, Nature changes, and it is different every single time — much like the experience of reading a book is different each time around.

WHAT ABOUT YOU? Do you consider yourself to be a flexible person? Do you find it easy to change plans? Can you deviate from your planned path? How does it feel when you change your itinerary or stray from your intended path? Does it make you feel out of control, disorganized, or something else? If this is something that you find difficult, would you like to be more flexible?

What about options? Do you usually take the time to see all the options you have available to you, or do you impulsively choose the first that you see? How would you feel about taking more time to make your decisions? And how do you make your decisions: with your head or with your intuition?

4

WINDMILL HILL SYCAMORE

One of the most special places in the world to me is Avebury, home to the largest megalithic stone circle in the world. Unlike Stonehenge, where the stones are blocked off from the public, you can walk right up to the stones at Avebury and connect directly with them: you can touch them, smell them, and feel their energy. It's considered by many pagan traditions to be a sacred site.

The surrounding area is full of ancient sites in all directions, including Windmill Hill, a classic example of a Neolithic causewayed enclosure, and also the largest site of its kind, made up of three concentric ditches. It's known for being one of the first ancient sites to provide evidence of the life of early farming communities, and it was excavated and preserved by Alexander Keiller, as was much of the Avebury World Heritage Site. Windmill Hill dates back to around 3675 BCE, and it's estimated that it remained in use until about 2500 BCE.

The day was clear and windy. I parked in the National Trust car park and walked through Avebury village, passing several red brick cottages and continuing on through the churchyard of the St James Church, which dates back to around the year 1000 AD. Not pausing to enter the church, which I had visited many times before, I headed down the narrow footpath that bordered a pretty cottage garden and led to a wider, paved pathway beyond. I followed the path, which was signposted as part of the White Horse Trail, as it went down the side of some rather large houses to my left, then past two benches on my right.

At this point, I paused to look at Silbury Hill, the largest manmade mound in Europe, in the distance off to my left. I never tire of that view: the large, conical, almost volcano-shaped mound that rises abruptly above the surrounding farmland. Why had the ancient people of this area dedicated an estimated eighteen million man-hours — the equivalent of five hundred people working for fifteen years — to build this mound? No one knows, and excavations have proved fruitless in discovering its secret. What's likely, according to experts, is that fewer people were working on the project over a much longer period of time and that the monument was constructed in stages.

Where the footpath forked, just beyond a little bridge, I turned right, then immediately climbed over a stile with a fingerpost sign marked "Windmill Hill" and continued onward. Crossing the field, I walked over a little wooden bridge and into a second pasture, which was also devoid of farm animals. Several empty fields and several stiles later, I came out onto a wide bridleway, where I turned left, still following the route of the White Horse Trail.

From there, the path slowly and gently climbed up toward Windmill Hill on a steady slope. Open fields of grain lay to my left; the path was bordered with trees and shrubs to my right, with more rolling fields beyond. I was so close to the Avebury stone circle, and yet I felt so far removed from everything. I always made it a point to visit Windmill Hill on my monthly trips to Avebury, and I rarely saw another person there. It appeared that local dog walkers were the only people to frequent the hill. It's the perfect ancient site to visit in peace and quiet: Windmill Hill is close to Avebury, but it is only accessible on foot, so few of the tourists who visit the stone circle make their way up the hill. Plus, at first glance it's less spectacular than the circle of standing stones, so I doubt it generates much publicity via word of mouth. In fact, I suspect that most visitors don't even know it exists, despite it being featured on most of the information signs about the archaeological zone.

When I reached the top of the gentle slope, I went through a gate. I paused as I entered the site, deciding on which way to go, and then I walked around the tumuli — round barrows — that dotted the hill, climbing up and over a large barrow on the far side of the field before heading straight to a small wooded area beyond. Round barrows are a man-made burial mound, often surrounded by a ditch. In Britain, these usually date back to the early Bronze Age, though some date to the Neolithic Age. Windmill Hill is home to several of these round barrows, all of which have been excavated.

Windmill Hill Plantation, clearly marked on Ordinance Survey maps, is easy to miss: it's a tiny wood of mostly sycamore trees located on the far end of the ancient site. I was drawn to it on my very first visit to Windmill Hill when I was there with my friend Cara. I got a very clear message that I needed to spend more time there on a return visit, and since that day, I have visited the wood each time I go to the area. It's a place of very special energy, and I always have the sense that there's much more going on than can be seen with the naked eye.

The sycamore (*Acer pseudoplatanus*) is a fast-growing deciduous tree with a broad crown. It is native to the hills and uplands of central and southern Europe, though it has grown in Britain for at least 500 years, where it has now become fully naturalized. Sycamore can be invasive and has been known to dominate woodlands if it is left to grow unchecked. Its leaves can often be seen marked with dark blotches, known as tar spots, which are caused by a fungus. Sycamore produces winged fruits called samaras. *Acer* is a genus of trees and shrubs commonly known as maples, and sycamore leaves very much resemble those of some types of maples. In fact, it is said that in ancient times people would cut the trunk of a sycamore to drink the sweet sap that flowed from the tree.

This was my second day in Avebury; I had spent the previous night at The Haven, a local B&B that I loved. On my previous day's trip to Windmill Hill, I had made contact with a large sycamore that had told me it had a story, but that it wouldn't give it to me just then. I would need to return. I hoped that on this day I would be able to receive the tree's story. I walked up to the same sycamore, which rather than being a single-trunked tree, was made up of a cluster of smaller trunks.

It looked as though it might have been coppiced. Coppicing is a traditional method of woodland management in Britain and other parts of the world in which a tree is cut down on a cyclical basis, encouraging multiple trunks to then regrow from the original stump or roots. The purpose of coppicing is to take advantage of the ability of many types of trees to put out new shoots from their stump or roots if they are cut down. This allows the forester to not only make use of the wood from the original trunk but of the subsequent multiple trunks that are later grown.

However, after some back and forth with the very kind

Emilie from Woodland Trust, she suggested that it appeared to simply be a multi-stemmed tree, or that it was a number of individual trees that have grown too close together, which is apparently quite common. She explained that in the past, trees were often used as way-markers, and that of course distinctive trees such as this large, multi-trunked one are better for this purpose, as they're easier to recognize when you're lost. This multi-trunked sycamore was not the only one of its kind in this little woodland — another one, which called itself the Four Knights, would contribute to the book in a later chapter.

The multiple trunks of this sycamore had formed a sort of bowl-like formation in the center, and I often climbed up to sit in the middle of the tree. I asked permission to enter, waited for the tree's affirmative answer, and then stepped up into the center of its clustered trunks and sat down, settling in to see if I could now receive the story. I had felt a bit unsettled the day before when the tree told me I would have to return. The sycamore began:

Yesterday, when you came, I said that I had a story for you, but not right then; and I know that you were disappointed, and I also know that you understood. I also know that it wasn't until much later that you understood why. You cannot simply — and I say this in the most respectful of ways — you cannot simply walk up to us and ask for the story and expect to receive. Even if we have told you that we have the story, we expect more from you.

We expect contact, communication, time.

You have heard from other trees about the importance of sitting, of being still, of engaging with Nature or observing Nature. Of being silent in Nature. And this is why I would not give you the story yesterday, even if perhaps the weather was better for us to do this yesterday — it is cold today, with a chilling wind — perhaps not the ideal situation in which you would want to receive a story, or in which you would even want to settle down and be still in Nature. And yet, you are protected: sitting in the midst of my trunks, for I am a multiple-trunked tree, as you can see. You are protected some, and we are not quite at the top of the hill, so the wind has not hit as strongly as it would if you were up higher.

Some say that I am a portal.

You have heard this yourself. A portal to what? A portal to other dimensions, a portal to the fairy realm, a portal to time travel, a portal to anywhere. You have not yet experienced this; it is not time for you to experience this, but it is possible for you to experience this... not today, but at some point.

You know that this is a special place.

The ancient people here used this hill as a burial ground for a reason — not just because it has a pretty view of all around. The hill was more wooded then; there were more trees, it had not been cleared for farming. And I know this because I retain the history through the network. You know that us trees have a network, but what you may not know is that generations of trees receive the information down the lines. And this is how I know what it was like back then. This is still a peaceful land, still quiet, still not very developed. But it was much more rustic back then, before agriculture had taken on in such large forms as it is today. There were no large herds of sheep grazing in this field, rubbing themselves against the barks of us trees to scratch. You see that the tree next to me has a whole section of its bark free from moss and is covered with strands of wool; it is because the sheep scratch themselves on us, and we are happy to have that type of engagement, that type of contact, that type of communication. We are happy to have living things wandering amongst us, and we are happy to serve as a scratching post!

Many people — well, not so many people — but some people do walk up here to this hill, because it is known as a historical point of interest. And yet very few people wander beyond the mounds, into this wood; which is disappointing, because we would love to have more interaction with the people that come here. In this wood you may feel a special energy, it is the energy of the fey; though you cannot see them, you know that they are here. And you are correct in guessing that that little wooded bit of trail, just to the side of this hill, is also a very special place. You can sense that you are not alone when you walk through that tunnel of green, and it is because you are not alone there.

Us trees see through all the dimensions.

We can see the human dimension and we can see the other dimensions as well; and that's how I know that you are not alone here, as you sit seemingly alone amongst my branches, amongst my trunks. The other dimensions overlap with this one. Sometimes you can see through, and sometimes you cannot. They can see through to yours. And they are always checking you out to see your energy, to see if they might reveal themselves, to see if they might step forth and communicate and step forth and connect, step forth and show themselves to you — they very rarely do this, because they know people do not believe. And they did in years past, hundreds of years past, but not so much now, and so they do not take the risk, which we think is unfortunate, but at the same time we understand; and we do not judge, we do not judge.

But if you sit silently, quietly, respectfully for long enough... and if you put forth the intention that you want to connect with them — in a respectful way — you might be just so lucky as to see them, and you might not see them in the way that you think you might see them. You might see them as clearly as you would see another human being, a solid three-dimensional being. Or you might see a shadow. Or you might see a flicker of movement in the corner of your eye. That is them. Or you might hear a sound — a sound that does not belong to a bird, or a hare, or a sheep — a strange sound. And you might find yourself looking behind and seeing nothing — that is them.

Some of the times that you are walking, when you are walking alone, and you get the sense that there is someone there and then you turn and see no one — that is them. They are coming forth to see you, coming forth to observe you, coming forth to evaluate you; but yet not coming forth strongly enough, confidently enough, visible enough for you to really know that they are there. And that is fine. And that is all right.

I don't know what kind of story you were expecting today.

I know that every tree has given you a different story, but I think it is my responsibility to tell you these things about the unseen realms — the unseen dimensions — so that you can know you are not alone, even if it looks like you are. And this is why humans — particularly small humans, young humans, children — enjoy fairy tales, because they still feel that sense of magic that can exist in the forest, even if as adults they may not believe. And I think that this is our job, you and I, to remind them that if they just opened their minds to the possibility, to the possibility of magic — to let in that magic into their lives — that they might start experiencing it in unexpected ways, in pleasant ways.

But to do this, you must respect.

Respect Nature, respect their world, respect the woods, respect the trees, respect the plants, respect the flowers, and respect the animals. So many people come tromping through the woods as if they were entitled to walk here, because it is a public footpath, and so they walk confidently and boldly through this land as if it was theirs. They step on flowers, they step on plants, and they break tree branches. These are the people who quite possibly will never connect with the unseen realms because they lack respect. Pay attention to where you tread. Pay attention to the soil beneath your feet. The rocks. The stones. The plants. Pay attention to the trees that you pass, the shrubs, and the streams.

Connect, connect, connect, and this will help you to connect with the unseen — because it is there. It is there, even if you think you cannot see it. There is layer upon layer upon layer of dimensions that you can connect with, and that you can benefit from connecting with. And we encourage you to do so. We encourage you to open up to the possibility. We sense that sometimes humans may be worried: what will other people think of us if we believe in magic? If we believe in the fairies? If we believe in the Nature spirits? If we believe in the guardians of this land?

You do not have to talk about it. You do not have to tell people. You can simply connect when you are out in the woods for a walk. And you can share the experiences if you choose. But we invite you — just you — you who are listening to this story, we invite you to open up to the possibility — if it is something that interests you of course. If it does not, then bypass my story and move to the next one.

But, we suspect that if you have been reading or listening thus far, it is because you are interested, and so we invite you. Slow down. Sit. Connect with Nature and open your mind.

And do not expect it to happen the very first time that you do this, because slowing down, sitting, connecting, connecting to Nature, opening your mind to the possibilities, it is like...your scientists would say it would be like strengthening neural pathways. We would say that it is like strengthening that connection: strengthening that connection between the known and the unknown, the seen and the unseen; the magical and the not so magical. The human and the fey.

The more that you strengthen that connection, the more likely you are to experience something magical, something new, something exciting, something unexpected — unexpected in a good way.

And so, we leave this with you now — with these words of encouragement. Sit. Be still. Be quiet. Connect. And keep doing so.

That is all.

I FELT a bit ashamed for having behaved so disrespectfully toward the sycamore on the previous day. I had asked permission to enter its cocoon of trunks so I could sit down, but I hadn't been very gracious in asking for the story that I knew it had for me. In the previous year, I had begun to ask permission to enter certain sites that I felt to be sacred, but I sometimes forgot to do so. My intentions were good, but I often lacked the formality of expressing them, and I probably came across as quite rude to the Nature spirits on many occasions.

I had indeed been told by my friend Sara that one of the trees in this wood was a portal tree, and I suspected that it was this very sycamore who was the portal. I wasn't fully sure what this meant, or what I might experience there, but I was curious. I was very pleased that the tree had confirmed what I suspected...and I was very interested in learning what I might encounter there in the future.

It was not surprising to me that the sycamore confirmed my other suspicion that I was not truly alone when visiting the wood, or when walking down the nearby footpath beyond. I know that I have asked you to keep an open mind when it comes to hearing the stories of the trees. Perhaps it has been a leap of faith for you to consider that trees might have a spirit and that their spirit might have tales to tell.

And perhaps it is an even bigger leap of faith to believe in fairies, or Nature spirits. As children, we might have believed in them, in the same way that many children believe in Santa Claus. And then we get to an age when many of us — the vast majority of us, perhaps — lose faith in the existence of these Nature spirits. Whether you call them fairies, faeries, fey, or fair folk, they are the magical spirits of the woods. You may also have heard them referred to as elementals: gnomes, or earth spirits; undines, or water spirits; sylphs, or air spirits; and salamanders, or fire spirits.

Whether you choose to believe or whether you prefer to remain skeptical is up to you. If you've spent enough time alone in the woods, though, I'll bet you've had a moment — or many — when you've been absolutely sure you're not alone, and yet there's no one around that's visible to the naked eye. I know I have, and the very clear tap on my shoulder when I was alone with the yew trees in the Chalice Well Garden at night is a perfect example.

After this tree's story, I became much more mindful of where I placed my feet when out walking in Nature. Walking on a public footpath, which is often worn down by foot traffic, is one thing, but when walking through woodland, where there are often little plants and living things, is another. I became more careful about where I stepped in these places, apologizing if I misplaced my foot and carelessly stepped on a living green thing. I became more engaged with my surroundings, and my sense of respect for all the living things grew as I did so.

I also became more aware of voicing my respect for the woodlands and for the sacred sites that I visited. I asked permission more frequently. I paused to take in the energy of a place before tromping boldly forward. I became more respectful.

~

HOW ABOUT YOU? Do you believe in a multidimensional reality? The concept of multiple universes or parallel realities have been explored in science fiction and fantasy, and also in the world of science. It was in 1952 that Nobel prize-winning Austrian physicist Erwin Schrödinger first shared this multiverse theory, which has had many modern scientific proponents, including Stephen Hawking and Neil deGrasse Tyson.

And how do you feel about the possibility of the existence of Nature spirits, such as fairies and other elementals? Do you think it's possible that these beings exist, either within our own dimension or outside of it? Are you open to the idea of setting the intention to connect with these beings and see what happens? Or would you rather just leave them alone for now, and hope that they do the same?

5

ALTON PRIORS YEW

Very near the Avebury World Heritage Site, less than fifteen minutes by car, lie the sister churches of All Saints Church in Alton Priors and St. Mary's Saxon Church in Alton Barnes. The two churches are about 100 meters apart, just barely visible from one another until you peek through the leafy oasis that borders the little stream running between them. Both are worth a visit and both are located along the White Horse Trail. They are accessible by car or on foot.

The tiny Saxon church of St. Mary's in Alton Barnes is still a place of worship for local villagers. The church door is usually unlocked and open to visitors, though it has been closed at times for restoration or to protect the church from vandalism. St. Mary's, with a roof dating to the 16th century and the pulpit and pews dating to the Georgian period, has undergone much restoration work over the centuries. Its churchyard is home to some beautiful ancient yews, though they are not as old as the more famous yew of the neighboring church.

The little All Saints Church of Alton Priors is perhaps best known for its 1,700-year-old yew tree, its age confirmed by a certificate from the Conservation Foundation which is located just inside the door. The Alton Priors Yew is visible as you enter the churchyard, down the right-hand side of the church. It's so old that its trunk has split into two, yet the tree grows on. You can even enter the sheltered space between the two halves of the trunk and sit or stand inside the yew. It's big enough for two people to comfortably sit within the tree — one in each half — without damaging its trunk.

The church itself dates back to the twelfth century and is a Grade II listed building that is now in the care of The Churches Conservation Trust. It's a place of extreme peace and quiet: I have visited this church on several occasions, and only once or twice have I crossed paths with another person there. The church door is usually unlocked and open to visitors, though the church is no longer in use for regular Sunday services. Unfortunately, the old pews have been removed and were replaced with simple chairs, but it's still a lovely place to visit and to enjoy a quiet moment.

This is yet another place of very special energy, and there are two indications that this may have been an ancient sacred site: the ancient yew tree, which predates the church, and the sarsen stones underneath the church floorboards that can be viewed by lifting up the two trapdoors. It appears that this is still a place of pilgrimage for some, as you can find feathers and crystals left as offerings on top of the sarsen stones.

Nearby the church is another reason for a pilgrimage to this site: Broad Well, a natural spring that bubbles up in a bend in the stream that runs in between the two churches. It is considered by some to be a sacred spring and it was mentioned as early as 825 in the Saxon Charters. You may have to walk around a bit before you find the spring as it's not marked in any way, but once you do, it's a very relaxing place to stop and watch the bubbles come up in different places through the sandy stream bed.

It was raining on the afternoon that I chose to see if the Alton Priors yew had a story for me, and I went straight to the tree, not stopping to visit the spring on my way there, as I sometimes did. I was grateful for the shelter the yew provided as I settled down inside the protection of its huge trunk. It didn't take long for him to begin:

You are safe here. You are dry here. You are safe from the rain. Safe inside my trunk.

You have seen the sign inside the church. You have seen the official notice — the certification that I am 1,700 years old. And though many people doubt this, it is true. Or at least as true as I know it to be in my interpretation of your human years.

I have stood here for centuries, and centuries, and centuries. And I have seen the changing of the landscape. Though I must say I am pleased that this area has not changed greatly. It is a very quiet village. Twin villages with their twin churches. Things could be worse: things could have changed more.

My trunk is old, old, old, old and it is split in two. This is what allows you to come inside and rest within my trunk.

Twin trunks, like twin churches, twin villages.

And this was a sacred place since far before the Church was here. This was a sacred place always. You can feel the energy here. You can sense the specialness of this place.

This feels harder to you, harder than telling the stories of the other trees you have spoken with. I understand why. Because of my size, because of my great age, it seems as if my story will be more important to tell than the stories of the other trees. And so, this blocks you, this trips you up. It makes it more difficult to tell my story, and yet my story is not more important than the stories of any of the other trees that you have spoken with, and that you will speak with. And that is because, as you know, we are all connected with our network. Our stories are passed down from generation to generation — and so even if I had not survived these 1,700 years, I would have this knowledge. I know that my age is almost impossible for you to grasp: the idea of a tree — one single tree — being alive for that many years. Seventeen centuries...170 decades. This is many, many, lifetimes for you humans.

It is difficult for you to grasp, and yet so many people are drawn here to this Church — to see me. And I am happy to have survived this long. I am happy to thrive. I am happy to have lived this long. I am happy to be an attraction, a focal point, the thing that draws people to this place, to this sacred land. And I wish that more trees could survive to this age, because people respect this age. People respect the years that I have been on this planet...and I can only wish that more people respected other trees in the same way.

I am not valuable simply because I have been on this Earth for 1,700 years, I am valuable because I am part of Nature, because I am a tree, like all other trees, like all other plants, like all other shrubs, like all other elements of Nature, we all deserve respect. And as I was saying, I do not deserve more respect. My story is not more important because of my age, because we have this network — and all of the trees that you speak with will have access to these ancient stories because they have been passed down from generation to generation.

You must seek out other old trees, other ancient trees such as myself, and visit them and bring attention to them so that people can visit them; because I sense that, as I have said, people respect age. They respect the longevity of a tree such as myself, and if people can visit ancient trees and have that sense of awe — that sense of respect — sparked in themselves, it will generate — perhaps, perhaps not — but it is my hope that it will generate respect for all the other trees and all the other living beings and all the minerals of this world.

Sometimes it seems that it is a miracle that I am still alive. You look around at the inside of this cave that is my trunk; I have split into two, which they say is normal for a yew of my age.

You are finding this difficult, and that is all right. As the very first yew that you spoke with told you, trees have stories, and for us it is important that our stories be told. This is a start. There will be many opportunities to get more stories, to get different stories, to get bigger stories, to get longer stories, to get shorter stories. This is a start.

If you think back to what was going on in this land 1,700 years ago, it will give you an idea of just how long I have been here. All of the things that have happened as I have stood, silently, patiently, quietly, in this churchyard, on this land, even before the church was built. The things I have seen, the people that have passed. It is a quiet place, there have not been all that many people, but it has been a long, long, time.

People back then had more respect for the land, had more respect for the trees, they had more respect for what Nature has to give. And they did not take without giving back. There was a give and a take. There was not the sense of entitlement that seems to exist today. The sense of: "this land is mine and I can do what I want with it." There was more respect, and I miss that, having seen the changes in attitudes. It is a quiet village. Nothing much has happened here, but I can sense it in the energy, in the thoughts, in the attitudes of the people that walk through here, of the people that visit — that things are different, things are very, very different than they were when I was a sapling, just starting to grow out of the ground here. Things have changed.

And I do believe — we do believe — that things can change; not back to what they were, because that can never happen, but they can evolve in a good way. And we can pick up some of what was lost. We can regain some of that respect, that love, that connection with Nature. It is possible. There can be a sort of revival of that connection with Nature, of that respect for Nature, of that belonging with Nature, of that co-existence with Nature. And people can release that sense of entitlement, of dominion, of power, over Nature; because as you have seen, Nature has great power as well. The power of the wind, the power of the rain, the power of streams and rivers, the power of earth, and the power of all living beings.

And sometimes this power of Nature is more than what humanity can handle and sometimes disasters happen. Things can go both ways. But I believe we can reach a place of harmony once more. A place of interaction. A place of working together. A place of harmony. Mutual respect. Connection. Deep connection.

I do not know if I will live to see that day, but I hope that I will. I have lived 1,700 years, more or less, and perhaps I will live 1,700 more — though I doubt it. That would be quite long for a tree, wouldn't it? But I trust that things will reach that point of harmony.

That is all.

THE ANCIENT YEW was correct in saying that I found his story more difficult to channel than some of the others. And he was also right in saying that his story was not more important than that of any of the other trees I spoke with: because of their vast network, each tree spirit was giving me a story that came not just from their individual experience and wisdom, but that of the generations and generations of trees that had come before it. The value of a tree's story did not come from the age of that individual tree, but of its lineage: hundreds and thousands of years of tree wisdom.

Because we humans live such short lives — short, at least, compared to the lives of trees — it's sometimes difficult for me to comprehend just what each tree has seen in the passing of history. If it is true that this yew is 1,700 years old, then it began its life somewhere around the year 318. At this point in history, Constantine the Great, the first Roman emperor to adopt Christianity, ruled Rome. The Chinese Empire lost its territories to the north of the Yangtze River. Later in that century, Mayan warlord Siyaj K'ak' conquered Waka, Tikal, and Uaxactun. These are all ancient civilizations. It's a massive understatement to say that this was a long, long time ago...and yet this yew was alive during those events. Pause for a moment and think about this.

While the Alton Priors yew doubted that he might continue to live another 1,700 years, that would not be an impossible feat. There are a handful of yews in Britain that are thought to be upwards of 3,000 years old — some individuals as old as 5,000 years. Let's think about what was happening thousands of years ago: in 3200 BCE, the Newgrange passage tomb was built in Ireland. In 3000 BCE, construction began on Stonehenge. In 2600 BCE, the written word was developed in Sumer and Egypt, which was a massive turning point in the course of humanity that signaled the beginning of recorded history. In 2500 BCE, the mammoth goes extinct.

It's a great stretch of the imagination to think that there are trees alive today which were also alive for those world events. A British yew tree that was alive during the same year that the mammoths walked this planet? It sounds impossible. Yet, according to estimations, there are indeed yew trees alive today that are that old. What might be happening in our world 1,700 years from now — in the year 3700 or thereabouts? Will humanity have recovered the deep respect it once had for Nature by then? Will humanity even exist then?

It's humbling to sit in the presence of such an ancient being. And yet, as the yew himself said, his value is not due to his age, but simply because he is a part of Nature. However, because we have such great respect for age, perhaps it is useful for us to seek out and visit these ancient trees, to spark our own deep respect for the living beings of the plant realm. His tale did make me reconsider my stance on connecting only with the trees I passed on my walks, rather than purposely seeking out ancient trees. Several of the trees in later chapters are old oaks from Savernake Forest, which is known for its ancient woodland.

WHAT ABOUT YOU? Do you feel that a being is due more respect simply because it is older? Or do you believe that all beings deserve the same respect simply because they are alive and are a part of this world? Do you believe something else entirely?

Do you hold the same hope as the Alton Priors Yew for the future of humanity's relationship with the natural world? Do you think we can rebuild a new sense of harmony with Nature? Do you have hope for the future of our planet? How long do you think it might take us to regain a deep sense of respect for and connection with Nature? How many generations will it take us?

Finally, do you know of any ancient trees in your local area? They don't have to be thousands of years old, but you can seek out a large, old tree to connect with. Do you have one in mind? If so, visit it. If not, keep an eye out for old trees on your walks. And if you know of a tree whose age has been estimated — like the Fortingall Yew, for example — then do a little research to see what was happening in the world around the time the tree began to grow.

6

WINDMILL HILL HAWTHORN

On yet another of my monthly trips to Avebury and the surrounding area, I headed straight up to Windmill Hill. It was windy, as it often was at the top of the hill, and I put on my windbreaker after climbing to the top of one of the round barrows and settling down for a rest. I sat in silence for a few minutes, watching a hare dart around the field, zigzagging through the grassy land, and then stopping now and again to pause and look around. It was aware of my presence, often staring straight at me, though I was sitting still on top of the tumulus. Once the hare had disappeared off into the distant farmland down the hill, I pulled out my journal and started writing.

It was hard to believe that I had first visited the Avebury area just two years prior when I walked the Ridgeway National Trail in 2016. The Ridgeway, an 87-mile trail, runs along an ancient trackway of the same name which is known as Britain's oldest road. It stretches from Overton Hill near Avebury at the southwestern trailhead to

Ivinghoe Beacon in the Chilterns at the northeastern trailhead.

On that first visit, at the start of my Ridgeway journey, I fell in love with the Avebury area — so much so that the following year, I began visiting it every other month for day trips, walking around all the ancient sites, often doing a circular route that I had found in my Ridgeway guidebook. About midway through 2017, I stayed at a B&B that I quickly fell in love with, and my visits to Avebury became even more frequent. In 2018, the year that I wrote this book, I visited at least once a month — sometimes twice — for one, two, or three nights at a time. I couldn't get enough of the energy of this place.

Early in the year Sara, the owner of the B&B, whom I now considered to be a friend, told me that she was selling her house. I instantly expressed my interest in buying it, and thus began my (eventually unfruitful) scramble to get everything in order so I could purchase it. I felt so connected to this land, and I was positive that I belonged there. I loved the energy of her home and her garden, and I just knew that this was where I was meant to be. Much of my journal from this year explored my deep desire to move to the Avebury area.

On this particular day, as I sat on top of the tumulus, I finished journaling and looked up, feeling drawn to walk down the hill a bit near one of the concentric circular ditches. I put my journal away in my backpack, got up, and headed toward the northern part of the site. As I walked a bit downhill, I saw a lone hawthorn just beyond the field of round barrows. I had never ventured to this part of the site, and so I had never seen the hawthorn before. It was a small gnarled tree, almost hidden from the top of the hill. It was sitting on top of a small grassy mound. Its trunk and branches were sheathed with lichen, making it look old and scaly. Faded, tattered ribbons hung from its branches: it had been used by more than one person as a wishing tree, though clearly not in recent months.

Common hawthorn (*Crataegus monogyne*) is a deciduous tree native to Britain and Europe. These are small, slow-growing trees, reaching a height of 15 meters. Hawthorns typically live up to 200 years, though they can live much longer. They often appear to be shrub-like, and are commonly used in hedgerows, though they can also grow as a small tree with a single trunk, like this individual. As you may imagine from its name, the hawthorn is covered in thorns. Its pretty white (or sometimes pink) flowers are highly scented and appear in spring, developing into pretty, dark red fruits called haws in the autumn.

Hawthorn, also known as May bush — or Huathe, as the tree is called in Old Irish — is another of the twenty trees of the Ogam. The hawthorn is thought to symbolize purification and sacred unity, cleansing and chastity. The flowers, leaves, and fruits all have medicinal properties, and hawthorn is thought to have the magical properties of cleansing the heart of negativity and stimulating love and forgiveness, which is not surprising considering that the berries can be used to make a tonic for the heart. It is thought by some to be a tree of enchantment, protecting the fairy realm — in fact, a lone hawthorn was thought to mark the magical entrance to the Underworld, and fairies were thought to reside nearby. It is considered a serious crime to cut one down, and unlucky to cut off any part of a hawthorn, except in the month of May. It is also considered unlucky to bring the blossoms into the house. Hawthorn is often used as a cloutie tree, where people tie a ribbon on one of its branches as they say a wish or prayer. These trees are often found near sacred wells, where people may dip the cloutie — the rag or ribbon — into the sacred water before tying it to the tree.

Perhaps the most famous hawthorn was the Holy Thorn that grew on Wearyall Hill in Glastonbury. It is thought that the hawthorn sprang forth when Joseph of Arimathea landed at the Isle of Avalon and thrust his hawthorn staff into the ground, which took root. The thorn was cut down in 1653, was later replanted, and then was cut down once more in 2010. Its replacement was planted two years later, and was also killed. We can only imagine the terrible luck that the tree cutter must have suffered upon destroying such an iconic hawthorn.

The Windmill Hill Hawthorn, however, was thankfully alive and thriving. As I approached, I got the clear feeling that it had a message for me. I sat down at the base of its slender trunk and settled in to receive its story. The hawthorn spoke:

You are correct in saying that this is your place.

This is your home, this is your land, and this is where you belong. And in the same sense that this land is yours, this land is for you, you are for this land...everyone in this world has a land that is for them; where they feel connected, where they feel rooted, where they feel grounded, where they feel right, where it just feels like home. Regardless of whether they go out into Nature and connect with the natural land, some people may sense that one place is right for them, or not. But they can deepen that connection, they can deepen that relationship, they can deepen that deep sense of home by going to Nature around that place and connecting with it: connecting with the trees, connecting with the earth, connecting with the water, the sky, the wind, all of the elements.

Many, many, people have not yet found their abode, their comfortable place, their home, and their spot in the world. And this is sad — because everyone does have a place.

We understand that people make decisions based on the practicalities of life; whether that be finding a job, proximity to family, friends, other things, practical things; but we would suggest that if you have not yet found your home, your place in the world; if you could just travel, visit, go to the places where your heart guides you. Whether that be the next town over, the next country, or halfway around the world, if you feel drawn to a place: visit, experience, connect...and we understand that this sounds just a bit crazy, because again the practical brain comes in and says: I can't afford that, I don't have money for that, what if I want to go to a place that is, as you say, halfway around the world, and I just don't have the money. We would like to suggest, again, that you put aside the practical thoughts, practical ideas, practical solutions, the practical problems and simply allow yourself to dream.

If you have a place in mind, start connecting with it: by reading about this place, you can buy books about the place, you can read online, you can do searches, you can look at photographs, you can look at images, you can collect images, you can make a collage of all your favorite images of this place. And connect with this place on a digital level, on an intellectual level, by reading...and that will start the journey.

There is a reason you are drawn to some places.

And that does not necessarily mean that you have to move halfway around the world and live in this place — but perhaps, these are places that you could visit. And once you make the connection, you may find that it is easier, and easier, for you to visit these places; and it is easier for you to return to these places, and it is easier for you to connect and feel that deep sense of belonging. That sense of "I am home, I am here" that so many people crave.

And so, we would like to remind you, that perhaps this path starts for you by setting aside practical worries, and concerns and simply connect wherever you can by reading online, by reading books — connect, connect, connect. And perhaps you will find the ways, perhaps you will find the practical solutions, on how to get to these places and how to return to these places and how to perhaps one day even live in these places that you are drawn to. But it all starts with that intuitive nudge, that calling of the heart, as it connects to your heartland; to the place where you belong, to the place that feels like home, to the place of your abode, perhaps, perhaps not... but you will be surprised what happens when you answer that call.

And, we feel the need to point out — to recommend, to remind you — how important it is to be still, of the importance of being quiet, of the importance of experiencing. So, when you go to these places — these places that your heart is called to — do not simply rush through them like a tourist, do not book a five-day tour where you are rushing around on buses all day. Do not hike through the land quickly trying to get to your next destination; but simply stop, sit, relax, feel, hear, smell, touch, taste, experience... experience with all your senses.

Turn up the volume of your senses and turn down the speed of your being, the speed of your action taking, the speed of your movements, the speed of your actions.

Slow, slow, slow, slow, slow; and sense, sense, sense, sense, sense. Sense the warmth of the sun on your face. The coolness of the wind on your hands. The sensation of light changing as the clouds move. Smell the freshly cut grass - the good and the bad; smell the sheep dung - for they are here too. Hear the birds, planes, the wind... feel the firmness of a tree against your back. Feel the softness of the grass beneath your hand. Slow, slow, slow and sense, sense, sense.

Become treelike.

This is not the first time that you have heard this advice, but it is good to be reminded. It is always good to be reminded because this rushing around is a habit we see in many people; a habit that can be broken, but it helps to be reminded — in order to break these habits.

This is all.

I AM SO grateful for having found my place in the world. I spent much of my life moving around: a few different places in California, then Spain, Costa Rica, Mexico, Argentina, Chile, and finally England. I dearly loved each place I lived in at the time — and I love the area that I still live in — but in 2018 I became obsessed with moving to Avebury. In the end, it turned out that the house was not for me, and that is fine. I know that there is a reason for this, and I trust that it will all make sense in the future: my months-long obsession with moving to Avebury, and the end result of having to stay where I was. I'm still not sure where my life's journey will take me, but for now, I am thankful for the place where I live, and for the places I return to, time and time again: Avebury and Glastonbury. They are my heart places.

The Windmill Hill Hawthorn had very practical advice: do what you can to connect with the places you are drawn to, the places you dream of visiting. Though I live in one of my heart places, and I regularly visit the other two, I also have elements of these places in my home and my office, to remind me of them when I'm not there. I have crystals that I purchased in Avebury and Glastonbury sitting on my desk and on my altar, and I have photos of Avebury and West Kennet Long Barrow on my computer desktop.

WHAT ABOUT YOU: have you found your place in the world? Have you discovered your heart place? Are you living there, or is it a place you visit?

If you have not yet found your heart place, your place in the world: which places are you drawn to? Which places have you always wanted to visit? What parts of the world do you find fascinating?

Finally, what do you think of this advice to become "treelike"? Do you find it easy to slow down and sense the things around you? Or are you constantly moving, taking action, doing things?

7

AVEBURY BEECHES

On another trip to Avebury, I spoke with the cluster of beech trees in the southeast quadrant of the stone circle, just beyond the circle itself, at the edge of Beckhampton Road. I had first connected with these trees on my original visit to Avebury when I walked the Ridgeway two years prior. After spending the day exploring the stone circle and the National Trust museums, I had sat down under the protection of the beeches to have a quick snack in the drizzling rain before heading off toward my B&B in East Kennett for the night. I still had at least an hour and a half of walking to go, plus a planned stop at West Kennet Long Barrow along the way. I wanted to have a quick rest before moving on.

(As a side note, you may have noticed the difference in spelling between the village of East Kennett and West Kennet Long Barrow. Interestingly, there is a custom of spelling the modern-day villages of East and West Kennett with a double T, and the ancient historical sites of East and West Kennet Long Barrows with a single T. The River

Kennet is also spelled with a single T. I have respected that custom in this text.)

Despite the fact that it was late in August, it had been a fairly grim day, with intermittent rain, and the beeches provided a bit of protection from the elements as I ate some nuts and pulled my waterproofs out of my backpack. On my subsequent visits to the stone circle, I always remembered these trees with fondness: they served as a reminder of that sense of excitement I had felt when exploring a new place and when setting out on a new long-distance trail.

On this day, two years later, it was a windy August afternoon, and once again I had been out all day. I was tired and was just about ready to head to my car and drive home. I walked clockwise around the white, chalky trail that topped the bank of the southeast quadrant and headed toward the beeches. There was a fine view all around: seemingly endless golden fields off to my left, the ancient stone circle to my right, and the village just beyond. The sky was filled with huge, light gray cumulus clouds that threatened to unleash their rain upon me at some point. I was tired and ready to go home, yet I felt drawn to the cluster of beech trees just off the chalky bank on my left.

Common beech, or European beech (*Fagus sylvatica*), is a large deciduous tree, native to southern England and South Wales, and on continental Europe, it ranges from southern Sweden to northern Sicily. It's a large tree that can reach more than 40 meters in height, with a large domed crown. Its dense canopy casts a deep shade, and the earth below a beech forest is carpeted with fallen leaves and beechnuts, which prevent most other plants from growing there. Beechnuts, also known as mast, are edible in moderation and can be used as a nut substitute in cooking and baking and can even be used to extract oil.

The beech is not as long-lived as some of the other

species we've met in this book, typically living only 150-250 years. Its bark is a smooth, light gray color, making it an easy target for arborglyphs — the carving of names or other messages on a tree trunk. Interestingly, the modern English name of this tree — beech — is derived from the Saxon words *beech* or *boc*, which is the same origin for our modern English word for book. It seems that beeches were made for writing, as beech bark tablets were used in ancient times.

Beech — Eamancholl, in Celtic — is one of the trees of the Ogam, and forms a part of the forfeda, or the five trees that were added onto the original twenty. It symbolizes ancient knowledge revealed, such as old objects, places, and writings. Beech represents learning, wishes, and letting go of fixed ideas. It is thought to be connected to Awen, or Divine creative energy, and thus will enhance the flow of creativity. It is also closely connected with wish-making, as some traditions have people write their wish on a beech stick before burying it in the ground. As you will see, some of the Avebury beeches are used as wishing trees to this day.

These particular beeches rose high up above the stone circle and provided a shady place to sit and rest, just barely off the path that most people took around the Avebury stone circle. I walked down amongst the trees and settled in against the trunk of one of them, immediately sensing that they had a story for me. It was summertime, which meant that the stone circle was at its peak tourist season, and I felt a bit self-conscious about channeling their story as people walked past, just beyond the shady cluster of trees where I sat. It felt like this was the right time to receive their message, though, and one of the trees opened up immediately:

YES, the wind has died, just a bit, and you can take our story.

We know that there is nothing more beautiful than a tree, though perhaps we are biased. However, the tall brown or gray trunks; the textured bark of our skin; our green leaves which turn colored once a year. We know these things are beautiful and we take pride in being so striking — some of us more than others, but we are beautiful.

And what caught your attention as you were walking towards us were the ribbons tied on our roots, and you have seen the other cluster of trees on the other side, with ribbons tied on the roots and the ribbons tied on the branches. And you have seen that those trees have so many more ribbons than we do. We like the ribbons. We like when people come and place their wishes on us, and they use us as the catalyst for making their wishes come true, for making their dreams come true. We know that we play a role in this. We know that our energy is strong and grounded and powerful, and we know that we can help with this.

And we know that some people come here, and they tie a ribbon on our branches just because they have seen everybody else do it, and perhaps they don't truly believe that we can help make things happen for them. They do not necessarily believe that our energy comes together with theirs to help their dreams become a reality. And yet, if they were to become aware of this, if they were to understand this, if they were to acknowledge this, if they were to consciously ask for help, if they were to consciously harness the power of our energy, which is so deeply grounded, so deeply rooted in this earth...if people were to consciously ask us for help when they place their wishes on our branches in the form of a ribbon, their wishes would be so much more powerful. But they do not know this, and that's why we wanted you to share this story.

We love the ribbons, not because we think they make us more beautiful, because we know that we are perfect, just as we are. We are in Nature: we are strong, we are rooted, and we are grounded. We rise high above the earth.

We know that we are beautiful, and we know that we do not need ribbons to make us more beautiful. It is the wishes that we like — it is the wishes that we want — it is one of the ways that we can help humans. And we love this, we enjoy this, we want to be a part of this. We see this as a kind of play, a kind of way that we can help, a way that we can help people make their dreams come true. But, remember, the more you ask for our help, the more help you will get. The more you become aware of what you are doing when you tie a ribbon onto our branches, the faster your dream will come true, and the more help you will get. Because by asking for our help and by consciously calling in our energy it makes things so much stronger, so much more powerful, because that energy is amplified.

We thank you for coming to talk to us. We thank you for coming to take our story.

We are always here; we are always here to receive: to receive your ribbons, to receive your wishes, to receive your message, to receive your cries for help, your calls for help, we are always here, and we always will be here. Us, our ancestors, us and the trees that come after us, as our ancestors were here before us. We are here to help. We want to help. And we ask you that you please ask us for help.

That is all, thank you.

I REMEMBER my first visit to Avebury when I walked the Ridgeway. The brightly colored ribbons of the cluster of beech trees high up on the bank of the henge caught my eye as I walked around the stone circle. Later that afternoon, when I went on the National Trust tour of the stones, I asked the guide why people tied ribbons on the trees' branches, and he could not answer me. It was the first time I had seen a cloutie tree or wishing tree, and I didn't know what it was.

It didn't take me long to do a bit of research once I got back from my Ridgeway walk, and I discovered that this was a way of making wishes. From then on, I bought ribbons for this use. I would cut them into short lengths, and I made it a point to always keep some in my backpack. Whenever I went to Avebury henge or anywhere else that had a cloutie tree, I would make a wish and tie on a ribbon. There was a hawthorn on the way up Waden Hill in the Avebury area that was also used as a wishing tree, and I sometimes stopped on my way to West Kennet Long Barrow to make a wish. Once I discovered the Windmill Hill Hawthorn of the previous chapter, I brought brightly colored new ribbons to tie on its branches.

But, as the beech knew, I wasn't doing it consciously. I was simply making a wish and tying on the ribbon. I wasn't intentionally connecting with the energy of the tree to add more power or potency to my wish. From then on, I began to pay more attention when I made my wishes, speaking directly to the tree to ask for its help. It added a new dimension to my practice, and it made the act much more personal since I was speaking to the tree and asking for its help, rather than ignoring it entirely and treating it as though it were nothing more than a framework for ribbons to be tied to it.

WHAT ABOUT YOU? Have you ever seen a wishing tree? Have you ever made a wish while tying a ribbon on a branch?

What types of things have you wished for? What types of things *could* you wish for?

Did you ever realize that you might elicit the spirit of the tree to help you to make your wish come true? Do you think that might help you to make your intentions stronger?

8

FULBROOK OAK

There is a walking route I enjoy that goes from Farnham to Godalming in Surrey, which I first discovered in the book *Time Out Country Walks Near London, Volume 1*. It starts near the western trailhead of the North Downs Way in Farnham, meandering alongside the River Wey, and then passes through woodland and farmland before ending up once more alongside the River Wey as the route ends at Godalming. Despite being easily accessible with rail stations at both ends and despite passing nearby fairly urban areas, the walking route often feels very remote and removed from civilization.

It should not have been a surprise that one of the Fulbrook oaks would have a story for this book. The route goes through a big grassy field near Fulbrook Farm that is dotted throughout with ancient oaks which I always fondly remembered and looked forward to seeing, and as I approached the field on this day, I was certain that at least one of them must have a story for me. As I mentioned before, oaks are one of my three favorite tree species, though at this point in my journey I feel a bit guilty about saying that. It seems unfair to play favorites when this book has taught me how special each individual tree can be.

When I went through the gate at the edge of the field, my eye was drawn to a massive old oak just to my left, and I immediately heard the words: "I have a story for you." By now I had grown used to this familiar process: I would sense my awareness being drawn to a tree, which I would visually identify before I tuned into its energy. Invariably, it would reach out to me, saying "I have a story for you" or "I'm not in your book." The trees were very clear communicators, getting straight to the point, and as the year went on I was getting better at tapping into their messages. Whenever I felt my awareness drawn to a tree, I knew enough to pay attention. I had learned my lesson after I walked straight past the Juniper Bottom Yews from Chapter 3.

It was a gorgeous, sunny October afternoon with a clear blue sky and crisp autumn air. I had been out walking since the late morning, and I was about three-quarters of the way through my intended route. I was feeling a bit tired, as there were no benches or natural places to rest along the route, and I was looking forward to sitting down and having a rest as I received the tree's story. It had been a quiet day on what felt like a very remote trail, and it had been a while since I had last seen another person on my walk.

The land around the oak was lush and green, filled with a myriad of plants and grasses. I carefully picked my way through the greenery and then I circled around the tree, admiring its massive trunk. I found a comfortable place to sit down, shielded from the main footpath by the plants, then I settled in to receive the story of the oak:

~

You are right I am old; I have been here for many, many,

years. Hundreds of years in fact. I am not the oldest tree in this field: there are trees older than I, there are trees younger than I, but I am hundreds of years old. And I have seen the passing of time, the passing of time in this quiet, secluded, corner of the world. I have seen the poles put up, for whatever it is that it provides you — electricity, telephone — and the wires that string across this field. I have seen the road put in just on the other side of this fence. I have seen sunsets and sunrises, and I have been here for many, many, many years.

There is a public footpath that goes through this field, and so few people walk down it. It is not a popular trail, this is not a well-traveled trail. And the people who walk it, the people who do *walk it, do not stop to connect with us. They may stop to sit underneath the shade of our branches, to have lunch, to have a break, to have a snack. But they do not make contact with us, they do not connect with us, they do not feel us. They do not sense the importance of trees like us, they do not sense our power, they do not sense our age, and they do not sense how long we have been here on this Earth. How many generations of humans, how many have walked past us? Because we have been here for a very long time.*

People may walk by and think: "oh what big trees, what nice trees," but they do not see us as the grandfathers that we are. We have been here for a long time: we have seen, we have felt.

It is autumn now and our leaves are not yet falling from our branches, but they are about to. Our acorns are starting to fall to the ground. You can hear them as they strike the ground all around you. It is that time of the year again: time for us to go dormant, for us to lie still, for us to shed our leaves, and sleep. And to save our energy for springtime, when it all starts again.

We have seen so many of these cycles, so many of what you call "years": so many, so many, so many. So many springs, so many falls, so many winters, and we flow through the cycles because that's what we do: we have no other option. Not that we would want another option — we just do our thing.

We would, however, wish for some recognition.

Not because we need it, it is not an ego thing, it is a matter of connection, it is a matter of cohabiting — trees and humans — and living together on this planet, on this Earth. You see us as you walk on your walks, you see us as you drive down your streets, but there is little connection with us. And the connection with us, the relationship with us, has been lessening over the years. We, the grandfathers, can see this, and we can tell you this. There are fewer people walking, because you have other methods of transportation, and there are fewer people who take time to sit up against our branches, against our trunks, against the logs of our fallen brothers and sisters. Very few people who sit and touch the moss on our trunks, who stop to feel the smoothness, of our acorns, who stop to really connect with us...they are few.

And that is why we would like to encourage you, when you see an old tree, to stop and sit. Sit with your back against our trunk, make yourself comfortable, relax, connect, feel our energy through your back, feel our energy through your spine. Feel our energy. And, if you like, allow it to trickle into your body, to flow into your body, to envelop you.

And feel some of our strength, our strength that goes back for hundreds of years, our strength that has allowed us to grow to this impressive size. We are pretty impressive, I know that. We have massive trunks a broad branch spread, I see my brothers and sisters out here in the field, we are something to be admired but not just admired, we are also something to be appreciated.

I urge you to connect with us, to feel our energy, all you need to do is take a few moments out of your walk and just sit with your back against us. Feel the texture of our trunk, the moss. But most importantly connect with that energy, connect with that life force flow and allow it to flow through you. And see what you experience, see how it feels, give it a try.

Feel it in your heart. Receive.

I OFTEN TOUCH a tree with my hands when I make first contact, but I rarely take the time to really feel all the textures of a tree: bark, leaves, fruits. When I see a particularly mossy tree or stump, I'll often pause to stroke it before continuing on. I do like textures. But the Fulbrook Oak made me aware that I could do more to really experience the different tactile qualities of the forest.

Instinctively I often sit with my back up against a tree, but before this conversation with Fulbrook Oak, I did not do so consciously, connecting with the energy of the tree. When I do this now, I can feel the energy of the tree flowing into my body. I feel it wherever I'm physically touching the trunk. I now see this as just one more way to connect with trees: physically and energetically, in addition to connecting verbally.

The words "feel it in your heart — receive" came to me as I was getting up from my channeling, after I had received the main message of the oak. Since this day, I have noticed that when I sit or stand with my back against a tree, I can sense the life force energy of the tree flowing into my body through my back, more or less where my heart chakra is located. It's as though I can feel the back of my heart chakra being activated by the tree.

WHAT ABOUT YOU? Do you ever sit or stand with your back against a tree trunk? This seems to be a natural position for many people who sit next to a tree, simply because it provides a sturdy back support. Have you ever noticed any kind of energy flow through the back of your heart center? If not, pay attention the next time you sit or stand next to a tree and see if you can feel it.

9

PEPER HAROW YEW

Later along my journey from Farnham to Godalming, on the same day that I had received the story from the Fulbrook Oak, I passed through the quiet rural village of Peper Harow, home to the little St Nicholas Church. Located just off the busy A3, you'd never guess when you sit in the churchyard that it was so close to such a busy road. This tiny community is a haven of secluded tranquility. As I mentioned in the previous chapter, this is one of those routes that doesn't have many benches or natural rest spots along the way, and each time I have walked it I have stopped at a bench in the churchyard to have a cup of tea from my flask. It's really the only formal resting spot along the route.

The Church of St Nicholas appears to date from the early 11th century, though other sources state that it's been a parish church since around 1301. Sadly, the church is closed to the public outside of Sunday services to protect it from vandalism, which it has suffered in the past, so I've never been able to see the inside of it, except for online photos.

Much of it was damaged by a fire in 2007, and it has since been beautifully restored.

I have always felt that this is a place of special energy, though it wasn't until I did a bit of research for this book that I learned that Peper Harow — now a private residential estate with a public footpath running through it — is thought to have been considered by the Saxons to be a sacred site, and was possibly a place of pilgrimage. A holy well called Bonville Spring is close by, though it's located on private property and is not accessible to the public. The churchyard is home to an old yew tree which is thought to be somewhere between 600 and 1,000 years old, depending on the source.

The weather on this day remained absolutely gorgeous, with not a cloud in the clear blue sky. It was one of those crisp autumn days that are perfect for walking: no tedious wind, no annoying rain, and no tiring heat. Spring and fall were my favorite seasons for walking, as the weather is usually not too cold or too warm, but just right. It was absolutely lovely, and as I enjoyed my tea break I felt myself relaxing into the peace of the place.

As I rested, I sensed my awareness being drawn like a magnet to the ancient yew tree that stood off to my right in the middle of the churchyard. Its trunk was hollow in the middle, and ivy crept up its side. I felt that it had a message for me, and possibly a story for this book, and I wasn't surprised to discover that it did. I quickly finished my tea, put my flask away in my pack, and carried my things over to the yew, where I sat down beside its huge trunk. I was already calm and relaxed from my break, so it wasn't more than a few seconds before I started to receive its story, which was quite brief:

~

This is a big and beautiful estate; there are many old homes here. This church is old. But I have been here much, much, longer — longer than most people think that a tree can be around. I am a yew. We are capable of growing old. You can see that my trunk is almost fully split, and there is an opening in my center, big enough for someone to even climb inside if they wanted to, and you could, and that would be fine. My branches are old, gnarled, missing some leaves on some of them. I have been here since before this church was built, on this sacred site.

There is a sense of peace here, and you can feel it, many feel it. That is why this was considered a sacred site, this was why the church was built here, this is why the estate was built here, this is why people have come to this area. It is like a pocket of calm, and peace, and tranquility and I have presided over this area for many hundreds of years. Perhaps even a thousand...I do not count time the way people do. But I am old, and I have been here to see and to feel the peace in this area over the hundreds of years that I have been here.

I would ask you when you see an old yew like me, whether it is at a churchyard, or somewhere else, to stop, sit, relax, enjoy, feel the calm, feel the peace, soak up the energy. Often us old yews are situated in ancient sacred sites, sites that may have been forgotten or sites that have not been forgotten because the modern church was built. Either way, these places are special. These places are meant for you to come to, to soak up the energy, to feel, to experience. Close your eyes. Relax. Feel the sacred energy of this spot. Do not be bothered about how you feel about the church — this sacred place predates the church. If you disagree with religion, if you dislike it, or however you may feel, sense the energy of this place.

The church bell may be a bit jarring, perhaps unexpected. (The church bell had just begun to strike the hour, and it was a shock in the otherwise silent afternoon.)

Close your eyes and allow yourself to soak up this sacred

energy. There are benches, spots to sit. Enjoy. And see what you feel, see what you connect with here. See what you can sense here and see what it means to you. I invite you, not just here, but again wherever you see an ancient, giant, yew like me.

That is all.

THIS WAS NOT the first tree to speak of its location as a sacred site, and it would not be the last. It was heartening to hear the tree confirm my suspicion that it was a special place, and it made sense that my reasons for wanting to rest in the churchyard were more than just practical. The location had that sense of being an energy bubble, somehow existing separate from the surrounding land.

I don't know what it is that leads people to choose a particular site for worship. Perhaps it's a place of sacred energy or an intersection of energy streams. Or maybe it's because a ley line passes nearby, connecting the site with other sacred spots. Ley lines are invisible lines that are thought to connect certain landmarks, including sacred springs and other sacred sites. They usually pass straight through a number of sites in a straight line, kind of like an energy highway. The St. Michael's ley line, for example, runs in a straight line from Cornwall to Norfolk, starting at St. Michael's Mount in the west and passing through Glastonbury and Avebury. Interestingly, there is a white ley line post located on the Peper Harow estate, which has an inscription on the side: "May Peace Prevail On Earth."

HOW ABOUT YOU? Can you sense when you're at a sacred site? Why do you think these places were chosen for worship in ancient times? What is it about the energy there that you think draws people to these particular sites?

And what about ley lines? Do you believe in them, or do you think they're something that was made up to connect the dots of the numerous sacred sites that are scattered all over the world?

10

RANMORE MAPLE

When I first moved to the Surrey Hills, I set out to explore the local public footpaths. Little did I know that I had moved to an area rich in walking trails, but the more I walked, the more I got a sense of the richness and diversity of the footpaths in my area. The very first trail that I set off to explore, a small footpath just off one of the main roads in my town, ended up being one of my favorites: from one simple trail into the woods, I could access a series of parallel and intercrossing trails all over the hillside and beyond.

One of my favorite trails was a little winding path through the woods which ran parallel to the main track, yet was hidden from it by thick, leafy trees. The little wood had a magical feel to it that I didn't quite understand, but from the first day I discovered this hidden path, I always chose it over the wider, flatter, more comfortable main route. It felt cozier somehow, more intimate, with a closer connection to the trees that bordered the path, many of which were draped with thick growths of ivy. Most importantly, I rarely crossed paths with another person on this trail, as most walkers tended to prefer the main trail, which was wide, flat, and smooth.

One day, I felt drawn toward a large Norway maple tree located just off to the left of the path, near the edge of the wood. I approached it and walked a circle around it, feeling the texture of its bark. I found a comfortable place to settle in between its surface roots, and I sat down, resting my back against its trunk. It felt like a very special place. It was almost like a microcosm: I felt as though I were in a bubble of energy, so close to the little path, yet so far removed from it. It felt like a private little resting spot. There was a filtered view of a grassy field just beyond the edge of the wood, though I was sheltered from it by the branches of the trees around me. Birds sang from their perches in the trees above, and squirrels rustled in the leaves on the ground, then scampered up the trees.

As I relaxed in the protection of the tree's canopy, I noticed a large white rock nestled among its roots. Picking it up, I found a small geocache container underneath it. I opened up the container, looked through the logbook, and then returned everything as I had found it. I loved finding geocaches, especially when I came across them without actually looking for them. It was always a pleasant surprise.

Geocaching is an outdoor adventure game where participants use a portable GPS device or the Geocaching app on their phone to navigate to a geocache, which is a small container that has been hidden for the purpose of this game. They will always have a logbook in them, and some will also have little toys or trinkets. If you find one of the larger geocaches with trinkets, you can leave one of your own and take one from the box. While urban geocaches exist, many of them are located in Nature. I had discovered geocaching a few years prior and had used it as a way to get off my known paths and explore new places in my area. It was fun to seek out and find new geocaches, and it was always exciting to unexpectedly discover one that I hadn't even been looking for. The geocache at the base of this tree somehow made the maple even more special.

I felt drawn to return to this Norway maple again and again over the months and across the seasons, even visiting it late one night at midnight on Samhain, the pagan festival held on October 31st that celebrates the beginning of the darker half of the year. The Norway maple became one of my special places in the woods. I knew this tree would be a part of this book, yet I wasn't expecting to receive its story on the day I started out to connect with Grandfather Tree and The Grandmothers, trees you'll be hearing from in future chapters. But as I walked down the little woodland path on my way to The Grandmothers, it spoke to me, and I knew that it was time to receive its story.

It was early fall, and I rustled through the leaves that had already fallen from the surrounding trees as I approached the Norway maple. I walked straight up to it, gently touching its bark, and then I settled into my familiar spot at the base of its trunk. I sat with my back up against its trunk, looking out onto the fields beyond the edge of the woods as the maple began:

You were drawn to me for a reason. Years ago, when you were drawn off the trail, just a bit downhill, to sit against my trunk. There is a special energy here: you can feel it. It is a calm — a sense of peace — as the breeze rustles the leaves of the trees around us, and as it rustles my leaves, too.

Other people are drawn to me, not necessarily for this energy, but because as you have seen there is a geocache nestled amongst the roots of the base of my trunk, hidden by a big white stone. Some people come looking and never find it. Some people find it and then move on. And, occasionally, people will sit and stop and look through the woods at the field that opens up just beyond where we are situated.

I know other trees have encouraged you to sit and spend time, rather than hustling through the woods. I would say the same, but I do not want to dwell on the same topic, so I will add a little detail to it: rest awhile, under a tree. Listen to the birds. Listen to the natural sounds, and to the unnatural sounds — such as an airplane, or the train when it goes by.

Close your eyes. Many people are fearful of closing their eyes in the woods, and we trees do not know why. There are no dangerous animals here, only other humans perhaps. So what I would encourage, when you sit against the base of a tree, is to close your eyes. You, humans, are so, so, dependent on your eyes — on your vision — for sensory input, for information. I would encourage you to open your ears and relax and rest and take in all that you hear: even the sounds that you do not understand — especially the sounds that you do not understand. And I would encourage you to resist the temptation to open your eyes when you hear something, but you are not sure what it is.

Hear the insects as they buzz around you; the leaves rustling in the breeze; the birds in the trees. And note that the longer you sit still, the more sounds you will hear. The squirrels will approach, the birds will approach; all the living things that are mobile in the woods will cease to see you as a threat, and they will come forward.

Rest awhile amongst my roots with your eyes closed...and trust: trust that you are safe, trust that you are protected, trust that all is well. Rest a while with your back against my trunk and soak up the energy and the sounds of the life of the woods. It is autumn now: you can hear an occasional leaf falling, rustling against the floor — the soil of the woods — as it settles.

Enjoy the sounds, enjoy Nature, and enjoy the energy. And

again: resist that temptation to open your eyes. You may need to ease yourself into this experience. If you find it exceptionally difficult, you might set yourself a timer: of one minute; three minutes; five minutes; ten minutes; fifteen minutes; half-an-hour. Start with whatever feels like a stretch. And then each time that you go out in the woods you can extend that time; or, perhaps, if you are going out on a long walk, spend one minute against one tree, then walk a while; spend three minutes against another tree, walk some more; five minutes against a third tree...and onwards.

Stretch your comfort zone — stretch your limits — so that you can fully experience the woods, and in particular the sounds of the woods.

That is all.

IT IS true that we experience the woods — or anything, for that matter — differently when we close our eyes and open up our hearing to take in the different sounds of our environment. It adds an extra layer of richness to the experience. And yet I think it's safe to say that most of us avoid spending too much time with our eyes closed when we're out in Nature. I know I do.

Despite the fact that I have spent hours upon hours alone in the woods, I still find it difficult to close my eyes for any length of time when I'm out on my own. I live in southeast England: there are no bears, no mountain lions, and no wolves to attack me. The most dangerous animals are probably the adder (which I've never seen), the fox (adorable), and the badger (of which I've never seen a living specimen: I've seen their dens in the woods, but I've only seen actual badgers in the form of roadkill). In fact, when I did a search on Britain's most dangerous animals, I found a list that included the bee, the wasp, and the seagull, among others. Ah, the dangers of the seagull. As you can see, this is a fairly benign land. Perhaps our fear of closing our eyes in the woods is simply an instinct that we've retained from our ancestors of hunting and gathering days.

When I'm fearful of closing my eyes and relaxing on my own in the woods, what I'm most afraid of are other human beings. And yet I've never had an experience out in Nature that made me feel unsafe or uncomfortable. Most other people that I cross paths within the woods are there for the same reasons that I am: to spend some time outdoors. Every once in a while, I will see someone behaving a bit strangely, or someone who looks wildly out of place — once I saw a man dressed in a suit and tie coming out of the woods near my home — but nothing uncomfortable or dangerous has ever happened to me. And I spend a lot of time alone in the woods. In fact, I usually feel safer the deeper I go into the woods: there are fewer people on the paths, and while I often sense the presence of unseen beings or Nature spirits, I usually feel safer around the presence of green things than I do around others of my kind.

WHAT ABOUT YOU? Do you feel safe when you're alone in Nature? Do you feel safe enough to sit in silence with your eyes closed? Would you be able to keep your eyes closed, even if you heard a sound that you couldn't identify? How do you feel about the maple's suggestion of stretching your comfort zone so that you can expand your sense of safety as you fully experience the woods?

Do what you need to do to stretch the limits of your comfort zone in a safe — not terrifying — way. The Norway maple was wise in suggesting that you stretch your limits slowly, by taking baby steps. This is useful advice for just about everything in life: when we set big, scary goals it usually makes it easier to achieve them when we break them down into smaller steps and milestones. Step by step, we take action outside of our comfort zone and toward our goals. Even taking tiny, baby steps toward what we want to experience is better than staying stuck where we are.

Obviously, you must use common sense whatever you do and wherever you go in life, so if you genuinely do not feel comfortable meditating in Nature, bring a friend or a group of friends.

11

RANMORE OAK

There is a particular oak tree that I have always been drawn to, ever since I first discovered it. It's up higher on the same hill where the Norway maple is located — Denbies Hillside — at a gorgeous viewpoint that looks out over the Surrey Hills. From this point, you can see the town of Dorking down below, with the village of Westcott next to it, and Leith Hill tower perched high on the hilltops to the south. Everything is surrounded by green: green hills, green fields, and green trees. Even in the winter, when the trees are bare, the earth below is carpeted in green grass.

The oak stands alone on this open, grassy hillside. There's a larger wood off in the distance, and the North Downs Way passes by just a few feet away. It's a place where many people come to visit — to walk, to enjoy the view, or to sit on one of the many benches on the hillside — yet few people choose to sit next to the oak itself.

I first saw this oak as I came down a narrow path that traversed the hillside, then turned around a bend. When I paused to go through the kissing gate that separated one part of the hillside from the other, my eyes were immediately drawn to the tree. I walked straight toward it, touched its rough bark, and settled down to sit among its surface roots, with my back against its trunk. This had become a custom of mine: whenever I was walking on that part of the hillside, I would go to the oak and sit with my back against it in that exact spot. It started to feel very much like a friend, though surprisingly I had never spoken with it before I collected the stories for this book.

Much like the Ranmore Maple, I was not expecting to receive its story on the day that I did, though I had known it long enough to suspect that it would have a message for my book. We had a connection. I was heading toward the path that led to Grandfather Tree, and as I came up around the hillside and saw the Ranmore Oak beyond the gate, I knew that this was the day. I approached the oak directly as I usually did, walking a full circle around it and touching its bark. It was kind of a personal ceremony for me with some trees: a way of engaging with them before sitting down next to them, almost like when you shake a person's hand when you meet them or when you hug a good friend or give them a kiss on the cheek when you see them. I settled into my familiar spot among the roots at the base of its trunk.

It was a clear autumn day, the air crisp and cool, and yet few people were out walking. There were fine views all around, unobstructed by cloud or mist. As soon as I sat down, he began to speak:

~

WE HAVE HAD A LONG RELATIONSHIP. You were first drawn to me the moment you saw me, as you were coming up the hillside, walking through the gate. I am a powerful figure on this hillside; I am one of the oldest trees here, and I am an oak. You may have noticed that we oaks have a certain gravitas. People are drawn to us: they are drawn to our size, our energy, our strength, and our beauty of course.

And you have had some ups and downs here, sitting beneath my branches. You have had a difficult conversation with another person here and that led you to avoid me for some time. And I am here to tell you that trees are the perfect place for difficult conversations, for awkward experiences with other people...or with yourselves.

We are the perfect place to bring troubles and sadness — to bring difficulties, to bring stress — because we can take it on for you; and transmute and change this energy, this uncomfortable, this difficult, this negative energy, if you would call it that. We can help absorb it from you and release it into the ground and transform it into something neutral. And it is important that you know this, and it is important that everyone hearing this story know this; because we can help, we are willing to help, we will help. And if you know that you can do this — we encourage you to take your troubles to the trees and to do so consciously.

Sit on the ground against our trunks, or stand next to us and hug us, or stand up against us with your back to our trunk. You can put your hands — the palms of your hands — on our bark. However you choose to connect with us physically, do so. There is no right or wrong way to do this.

Imagine your worries, your troubles, your sadness, your stress — whatever it is that you have — flowing out of your body and into our trunk. Sense us absorbing that energy and then pulling it down, down, down, down the trunk, down into the roots, into the earth; and transforming that energy into something neutral. It is a process that does not hurt us: it does not hurt the earth, it does not hurt the planet, and it does not hurt anything, because we have this capacity to take what is troubling you and to transform it.

And if you do this consciously, it is all the more powerful. And if you do this on a regular basis, even better for you.

You can pick any kind of tree you want: you can pick a big oak; you can pick a yew; you can pick a holly; you can pick any plant, any tree you want. You could even pick a big shrub, but you might find yourself more drawn to the trees for this task.

To be fair, you could even lie down on the grass and visualize yourself sending this energy into the grass, or to the plants; but, because I am a tree, I would like to suggest that you try this with trees. You could say that I am biased in that I think we are the perfect plant life form to help you in this way.

Feel yourself now, settled in, sitting on the earth, leaning up against my trunk, your hand on the base of my trunk. You can visualize yourself sending that stress, sending that uncomfortableness, sending whatever it is that you want to release out of your body and into my trunk... out of your body and into my trunk. Out of your body and into my trunk, and see it flowing. Flowing like a stream of energy, out of your body and into my trunk. And then from there see it flowing into the earth.

You might want to visualize it coming out of your body a particular color. It could be red, or it could be something else: brown, black or white, whatever works for you. And then, perhaps, as you see that energy flowing out of your body and into my trunk and down my trunk, down into my roots, down into the earth, you may want to visualize that energy changing color as it flows.

If you sense a darker color coming out of your body you may sense it turning lighter, and lighter and lighter and lighter. And as it flows away into the earth, you may sense it turning into a bright, white light of energy, disbursing into the earth beneath you, into the earth all around you and spreading out as this neutral energy that has been transformed and transmuted and changed by the power of Nature, by the power of the trees; and by the power of you being willing to do this work. So this is what

I ask you: bring your troubles to the trees. We will take care of them for you.

Thank you, thank you, thank you.

This is all.

It was true that I had avoided my beloved Ranmore Oak for some time. The memory of that conversation had become anchored to the location and to the tree itself, which meant that I didn't want to be reminded of it by visiting the oak. For years, I would often walk by it, but I would no longer stop to rest there. I would hurry on past, not pausing to visit with the tree. It felt as though that one conversation had ruined my relationship with this oak.

But in reality it was exactly the opposite: I now understood that the oak had been the perfect location for that difficult discussion because it had helped me transmute the negative energy of the situation. At the time I had been unaware of the oak's role in helping me through a difficult day, but it had been assisting me, nonetheless. Now that I knew the trees were capable of providing such support, I would be able to actively engage them in helping me through difficult times and emotions. The story of Ranmore Oak made me wonder about all the other ways that plants and trees could assist us through troubled times that we weren't aware of. There were so many ways that we could work in partnership with the plant realm to get help in times of difficulty, and I sensed that I was only just beginning to learn about them.

When I'm feeling excessively stressed or upset, I often want to go within: to crawl under the covers of my bed or snuggle up with a blanket and hide. It's not my natural reaction to want to go outdoors and seek help from Nature.

In fact, it's something that I'll have to remind myself to do. But I truly believe in the power of trees to help us in this way. And I intend to make it a habit to take my worries, fears, and concerns to the trees.

What I find interesting is that we often engage with trees and with Nature in unconscious ways: we tie a ribbon on a wishing tree; we sit with our back against a tree when we're feeling down. And thanks to these stories from the trees, we can now learn what's actually going on at an invisible level — what's happening at the energetic level. It's even more powerful for us to engage in these activities consciously: being fully aware as we take our wishes or our troubles to the trees. I think that adds a whole new level of depth to the activity, a new sense of power.

WHAT ABOUT YOU? Have you ever had a difficult conversation with someone when you were out in Nature, perhaps while sitting underneath a tree? Were you aware that the trees might be able to help you through your troubled times? How do you feel now about taking your worries to the trees? Do you have a particular tree in mind that you'd like to ask for help with this?

12

GRANDFATHER TREE

A couple of years ago, I was working with my business coach Lisa Wechtenhiser, a very clear channel who has taught me a lot about channeling and about developing a sense of unwavering trust in myself (which, as you may have noticed from the Introduction, is still something I'm working on!). In a session with Lisa, we were about to sign off the call when she got a very clear message that a specific tree wanted to connect with me. He called himself Grandfather Tree, and he asked that I go out to see him and speak with him. He said that I already knew who he was; I just needed to trust myself and seek him out.

As soon as Lisa said the words "Grandfather Tree," I instantly knew which tree it was. But I second-guessed myself: was it *really* that tree? I knew it was. But was it? I kept going back and forth.

I set out from my house a few days later and headed straight for the old lone oak that I knew to be Grandfather Tree, though I still questioned it. He, like Ranmore Oak, sits alone in the corner of a huge open field, bordered on the south side by a thick wood, and on the north by a little farmhouse and barn. He's an old oak with a majestic green crown that changes its shape a little bit with each year's growth. Rolling green hills lie beyond, and dark trees border the far end of the fields off in the distance. It's a magical, idyllic setting.

The little footpath that I always take to get to Grandfather Tree leads gently through Dorking Wood, exiting the forest to head more steeply downhill towards the farmhouse. As soon as I left the shelter of the trees, the landscape opened up and I immediately saw the old oak to my left, not far off the trail. I saw him, and I knew in that instant that he was Grandfather Tree.

I walked down the little hill and then went through the gate into the field where the old oak stood. As I approached him, he confirmed that he was, indeed, Grandfather Tree. I spent a few minutes talking with him — at this point, I don't even remember what about — and I sat against his trunk for a while. Then I got up, thanked him, and moved on.

Despite having received a very clear confirmation that he was indeed the tree I was looking for, I still questioned myself. As I walked through the woods on the north side of the field, a large tree to the right of the path caught my attention. I asked if it were Grandfather Tree, and it replied that I knew that it wasn't. "Why would you ask such a thing?" it demanded. It seemed annoyed with me. I thanked it, felt silly for not trusting myself, and continued onward.

After some time, I finally trusted my instinct — and the very clear messages I had received — that the lone oak was indeed Grandfather Tree. I returned to him from time to time, to talk or to sit in silence up against his massive trunk. He seemed a bit grumpy at first — perhaps because I had been so reluctant to trust myself — and for a very long time, I felt that it was hard to make a connection with him. But then, back in the day when I first started communicating with trees, I often sensed that big old oaks could be a bit grumpy, so this wasn't a concern for me. Time passed, and I learned to visit him in silence, sometimes with nothing more than "hello, goodbye, and thank you." I enjoyed sitting in his presence, but we didn't talk much beyond basic pleasantries. It was an awkward relationship for a long time.

On the day that I received his story, I was feeling more confident: I had already warmed up with the stories from Ranmore Sycamore and Ranmore Oak, and I was ready to collect more stories. I strode through the grassy field, thankful that the tall nettles that usually surrounded Grandfather Tree had been trimmed around the base of the oak, making it easier to sit down and relax without worrying about constant stinging. As soon as I settled in, he began to speak, much more eloquently and extensively than in any other of my interactions with him:

WELCOME BACK.

I know that I am one of the first trees that you made a connection with. I know I am the first tree that you specifically searched for and sought out a connection with.

I sent you that message because I knew that you needed the challenge of finding me — the Grandfather Tree — amongst all the other trees that you have passed on your walks. And you knew instantly which tree I was, but you still questioned yourself. You still questioned yourself, and you asked other trees if they were the Grandfather Tree, while at the same time, a part of you knew that it was me. And you have come back many times in the different seasons and you are here now connecting, learning, receiving.

I am here to tell you, and your readers, to trust. Trust, trust, trust yourself. One of the most important things that you can cultivate, in the inner garden of your mind, is a deep, deep, deep trust of yourself. And the reason why this is my message for you is precisely because you did not trust yourself when I sent the message that you were to find me — first you received the message not directly, but through someone else, and then you questioned who I was.

So, I am here to remind you — all of you — to trust yourselves.

It can be hard for people to trust themselves in this day: there are so many distractions, so many worries, so many stresses, and so much information. There are so many signals that you are receiving that it can be very, very hard to lower your antennae and to tune in to your inner self, your inner knowing, your inner knowledge, your inner wisdom. Tune into your own signals, your private signals, which circulate within yourself, within your body, within your mind, within your system.

Trust yourself.

There are many ways to do this. But the most important — the easiest — way, is to allow yourself to slow down, to give yourself permission to slow down. In general, in life — and also as you walk in the woods — allow yourself to take slower steps to walk at a more leisurely gait. Slow, slow, slow. And then sit: sit on a log; sit with your back against a tree; sit on a grassy field, sit wherever you want. Sit, and this does not even have to do with Nature: it can be done at your home, it can be done at your office; it can be done in a park; it can be done anywhere.

Sit in silence. You do not have to meditate, but you can. Just feel yourself slowing down, feel your thoughts slowing down, allow all the muscles of your body to relax, and especially your face: these can often be the last muscles that you allow to relax.

Feel yourself relax... and go within, whatever that means for you.

Slow down.

And allow any messages to come to light: messages from your inner self, messages that you need to hear. Allow yourself to spend time with yourself on a regular basis...slowing down... slowing down... slowing down. And allow yourself to receive from yourself. And slowly you will learn to look inward for advice, to look inward for wisdom, to look inward for a sense of direction.

Trust yourself. This is the biggest gift you can give yourself. And for your readers this is something that I would like to give you as a challenge: I call myself Grandfather Tree. I would like to challenge you to go out and find your grandfather tree. It could be a tree that you have already seen on one of your walks; it could be a new tree that you have yet to discover. Set the intention to find this tree and make contact with it and trust yourself that you have found the right tree, the correct tree, your grandfather tree.

This is all.

IT SHOULD NOT HAVE BEEN surprising that the very thing that I've learned from Lisa — unwavering trust — was the same lesson that Grandfather Tree had to teach me. And while I cannot say that I experience unwavering trust in every aspect of my life, I can say that my sense of trust in myself has deepened greatly over the years. I now have a deeper sense of true north, an inner compass that was lacking in the earlier years of my life. It's not always there, and sometimes I lose track of it, but for the most part, life is easy when I'm tapped into my inner compass of unwavering trust.

This has been a massive shift in my life: I've gone from not knowing what to do or what decisions to make, to having a clear gut feeling of what to do, when to do it, and how to do it. Again, this isn't something that I experience 100% of the time, but it's how I live my life *most* of the time. It's why I often say that my gut is smarter than my head.

A few years ago, I channeled a new energy healing and mindset-shifting process that I call Heart-centered Energy Work®. It works by reprogramming subconscious beliefs while at the same time shifting any energy blocks that might be present. It can be used to work on any type of fears, blocks, or limiting beliefs. The process, however, always starts in the same way: by balancing the heart center. When we do this, we set the intention of improving our self-love, self-acceptance, and self-trust.

Channeling the HEW® process required a deep sense of trust in myself. I received the method step by step, and I had to take action on each step, not knowing what would come next. It was a massive lesson in trusting myself enough to take each step one at a time, even though I couldn't see the whole path in front of me.

I share this with you because developing a sense of self-trust has been one of the biggest shifts in my personal development, and it's something that I wish everyone could experience in their own lives. That's why weekly done-for-you Heart-centered Energy Work®, or HEW®, is included in one of the most basic levels of my Patreon tiers. It's a core quality that I think we could all use in our lives, and I want to make it easy for people to develop it. There are many ways to achieve this, and this is one of the easiest ways that I've found.

When we trust ourselves deeply and completely, we know what's right for us. We stop looking outside ourselves for advice and guidance, and we first look within. There is a time and a place to get help from others, don't get me wrong, but it's incredibly empowering to first go within ourselves and check in with what we know is right for us, and then get help with the details.

WHAT ABOUT YOU? Do you fully trust yourself? Do you trust the decisions you make, or do you constantly second guess yourself? Do you feel that it's safe for you to trust yourself?

I encourage you to heed Grandfather Tree's advice and open yourself up to the possibility of deeply and completely trusting yourself. This is not something that most people will develop overnight; it's work that takes time. Give yourself permission to trust yourself, and you'll start down that path of inner development.

Grandfather Tree also recommends slowing down, sitting in silence, and becoming aware of the messages that float up to the surface of our awareness. While this is excellent advice, it can be hugely challenging for someone who isn't used to sitting in silence or meditating. Some years ago, I came up with something that I call my "mind decluttering meditation": in it, I grab a paper and pen and I sit in stillness as though I were about to meditate. I settle down, and quiet my mind. Instead of consciously letting go of thoughts as they come into my awareness — as I would when meditating — I open my eyes and write them down.

Often our minds are cluttered with things we have to do: something we have to buy at the store, a person we have to call, an email we have to send. Tasks. Actions. Errands. If we get these out of our head and into a reliable system, we can clear our minds of the clutter that prevents us from hearing the messages of our intuition. That's why the mind decluttering meditation is so useful: it cleans things up and it gives us the space to listen to the important stuff that's underneath.

Have you ever tried anything like the mind decluttering meditation? Do you tend to carry your "to do list" around in your head? If so, I encourage you to try this simple meditation to declutter your mind. You might need to do it more than once. You might need to do it every day for a week or two...or longer. But eventually, you'll retrain your brain to get your tasks out of your mind and into a system that will ensure that you get them done without taking up valuable brain space. And in doing so, you clear up your mental bandwidth, allowing your inner guidance to speak more loudly.

13

THE GRANDMOTHERS

Earlier in the year, I received an Akashic Records email from Vickie Young where my Records Keepers spoke of a very specific grove of trees called The Grandmothers. When I read the message, I instantly knew which trees they were referring to. Several years prior, when I first moved to the Surrey Hills, I came across a very special little grove. It caught my attention as a place of special energy, though I didn't stop to linger at the time.

As I continued to explore the hills and woods in the area where I live, I often had that special grove in the back of my mind. I had a general idea of where it was situated, but I wasn't sure of its exact location. Eventually, I set out on a walk with the specific intention of finding it, and as soon as I neared the little grove, just off to the side of a narrow trail, I knew I had found it. Since rediscovering this site, I've gone back many times to sit in silence and to visit the trees, and I once brought a group of walkers there to meditate and to experience the special energy of the place. I discovered that it wasn't just me — they felt it, too.

I'm not the only one who is drawn to this private little grove. Every time I go there, I see evidence that others have been there in recent days: I have found new graffiti on the bark of the trees, old abandoned tent poles, bottles, cans, and empty beer cartons. Once I came across an elaborate web of brightly colored yarn that had been strung up between two trees. Just beyond the grove, where the little hill slopes down into a gully, there are the remains of an old campfire which has clearly been used time and time again. Often I find large stumps and logs arranged in a circle within the grove. On more than one occasion I have gone there with the specific purpose of collecting rubbish and carrying it back home to be recycled or thrown in the trash. It appeared that many people enjoyed the secluded spot, but they didn't seem concerned with cleaning up after themselves when they were finished.

It wasn't until I received this Akashic Records email that I actually connected with the trees in this grove to receive their story, and thus deepened my relationship with them:

> *Holly, when you walk by certain trees on your walk, do you notice that some really speak to you? Of course, you do! :)*
>
> *We would like you to start to be aware of a certain grove of trees that you see often in your daily or at least weekly outside excursions. This grove is made up of the Grandmothers and they wish to pass knowledge on to you so you can share it with other women who have had the same personal power issues that you have bumped into in the past.*
>
> *This week take some time to walk alone to ask that they appear to you...or if you know who these Grandmothers*

are and where they are located, then please visit them. Sit with them. Share with them and then just listen to them.

This was a tricky story to receive. It took me weeks — no, months — to actually get out and connect with them. I kept the email at the bottom of my inbox where I could see it every day, as a reminder of what I needed to do. It nagged me in silence. Yet for some reason, I kept resisting this task, perhaps because I was afraid of what they might say. Or maybe it was because it seemed like a big, important message and I was afraid I wouldn't be able to receive it fully. When I finally went to see The Grandmothers, it was on the same afternoon that I received the stories of the previous three trees. I had been out walking for a couple of hours by this point, and I was tired. It was definitely *not* the ideal time to receive their story, and I ended up returning a few weeks later to receive the rest of it. That's why their message is shared below in two parts.

You are correct, we are the grandmothers.

You were surprised when you returned to us to see that we are not very old trees. But we hold the energy, and the connection, and the information, and the tales of the trees that have come before us in this grove, on this land.

You have been coming here for many years, and you can sense that this is a special place...and you are right. The energy here is special, it is different. And it draws not just you but other people, as you can see by the graffiti on our bark. You see the ring of stones where people will light fires at night. You see the litter, which you occasionally come to pick up. You see the abandoned tent poles. This place has long drawn all kinds of people: people with good intentions, who have respected us, and people who have used this place as a secluded site to drink. You can even see an empty carton of beer over there.

People come and go. We are glad to be visited. We are not glad to have people spray paint things on our trunks, on our bark. But we are glad to provide a place where people can soak in this energy, even if they do not understand what it is or why they come here.

This is a quiet place, with the exception of the train that goes by, off in the distance. Whenever you feel a place like this, sit and soak up the energy even if you do not understand why *it is that you believe it to be a special place. You do not need to understand the specifics. The fact that you sense the specialness of the energy is enough for you to know. And if you feel drawn to return to places like this, come back: as often as you can, as often as you want to, as often you choose to. Come and visit these special places in the woods.*

As you know, our story was not complete the last time, and as you know you are here to collect a story of personal power. The words that we gave you on your last visit were simply an introduction to the things we have to say to you. You were not ready to receive the full story the last time you were here, and that is why it was so difficult for you. It is why you had to return. We are glad that you have returned and that it is now time to transmit the message that we have for you. Personal power has long been an issue for you — and for many, many, other people — and this is something that we can help with.

We are trees. We are tall, and we are deeply rooted in the ground. Not all of us, of course: you see the young yew tree straight in front of you, some of her roots coming out of the ground, leaning to the side. We are not all so fortunate to have deep, deep, roots, but most of us do. We are standing tall, we are standing grounded, and we are standing strong.

When you think about personal power and what it means to you, we suggest that you think of the trees. Think of us Grandmothers, or of any other trees you have seen on your walks: in parks, anywhere. You know what a tree looks like, you can easily visualize one. And so we would recommend that you stand wherever you are, and you close your eyes. Feel roots coming out of your feet, going down into the earth. Down, down, down, connecting with the power and the energy of the planet Earth.

Sense yourself becoming a tree. You might want to stretch your arms up to the sky, as you envision branches growing out of them, branching off into smaller ones, leaves sprouting on them. As you grow and flourish into a deeply rooted tree, strong, and grounded, and beautiful with your foliage, really feel *what that feels like. Feel what it feels like to be a tree, just being* you. *Pick whatever type of tree you want: you can be a holly, you can be an oak, you can be a yew, you can be a beech, you can be a sycamore, an elder. You can be whatever tree comes naturally to you, whatever tree you feel most drawn to.*

And feel! *Feel that sense of being strong and tall. And you might want to speed up time so that you can grow and feel the girth of your trunk expanding, as new layers of bark grow on your trunk, and new rings form within you. And you grow stronger and stronger and more solid.*

Really sink into that feeling and experience *it. Stay here for as long as you need to, experiencing the sense of treeness, of* being *the tree, of* feeling *the tree, of feeling the* strength *of the tree, the* power *of the tree, the* energy *of the tree. Really feel what that feels like, and when you are ready to come back to the present moment, bring that sense of treeness with you, and this will help you tap into your own personal power.*

You can do that visualization as often as you like, as often as you need to, as often as you feel the need to, as often as you want to.

Personal power is a feeling *— like that feeling of treeness — and it is multi-layered. It is not something that most people will achieve overnight, or after one simple visualization. It is made up of the layers of self-trust, self-love, self-acceptance, self-esteem, self-confidence, self-value, self-worth. And it is the sense of all of these things being deeply grounded and connected with all the multiple layers of your being: your conscious mind, your subconscious mind, your superconscious mind. It is your regular everyday self, connected with your Higher Self, or soul, or whatever it is that you personally choose to call it.*

The more you can do to connect with all *these parts of you and to activate and amplify self-love and self-acceptance and self-trust, all of that work, this multi-layered, multi-dimensional work, will help contribute to your own sense of personal power. You can do this work in whatever way is natural to you. You can do your beliefs work and your energy work: you have so many different techniques and modalities and ways of working with this. You can do visualizations, like the tree visualization that I just shared with you.*

If you are feeling powerless in your life, know that many, many, people feel the same: this is quite normal, do not chide yourself for this, do not feel bad about yourself for this, do not feel like there is something wrong with yourself for this. Many, many, people — I would say most people, we *would say most people — feel powerless, or very nearly powerless in their lives, in their everyday lives. At the very least, they do not feel grounded and strong in their power. And yes, that is another thing that we are: we are strong — even that yew tree that is bending over, as her roots are coming up from the ground on one side. She is strong, her wood is strong.*

When you fully step into your personal power, you will feel *strong. Now, we recognize that some people may have fears —*

fears about power. Power can be such a dirty word, and some people have such a bad concept of power. Power is neither good nor bad: it is neutral, you can choose to step into your power and use it for good, or you can choose to step into your power and use it for not-good.

When we share these messages with you, we are sharing them with the intention that you will step into your personal power and use it for good, because there are so many good things that can be done. And there are so many good things that are not done, that are not happening because people are not choosing to step into their power. They are choosing to be victims. They are choosing to feel *small, they are choosing to* play *small, they are choosing to be invisible.*

Because power is scary sometimes. Sometimes it doesn't feel safe. It is unknown, maybe outside your comfort zone, maybe new to you. That's why we are here, we The Grandmothers: we are here in our grove to share with you these messages of personal power. And there are certain places in the woods, as we mentioned in the first part of our message here, where you might feel drawn to. And if you do go to these places, know that the trees can help you with your personal power; because we are strong, and we can help transmit that energy to you.

We recognize that this is a big ask, we recognize that this sounds like a big task. And we would like you to choose *power. You will know if this feels right for you, if now is the time. And even if it is not the time now, but you sense that it might be the time in the future to choose power, put your hand on your heart and say in your own words:*

> I choose power for the good. I choose to step into my personal power. I am ready, willing, and able to step into my personal power and to live a life where I am grounded in my personal power, which I choose to use for the good.

Make that statement to yourself, to the universe, to the trees, to your world. And start doing the work: start doing the work to call back your power, to feel *your power, to understand that power can be used for many, many, many beautiful things. Power can be good. It is neutral, and it is* how *you choose to use it that matters. And the more people that choose to step out of powerlessness and hopelessness and victimhood, and step away from those things and into their personal power, the better. The more people that choose the path of personal power for good, the faster this world will transform, and the more people that use their personal power for good, the more this good will be amplified, and that energy will crowd out the people who are currently choosing to use their power for not-good.*

So we encourage you to make your statement, to take your stand — even if you feel you are not ready. This may not feel comfortable to you. It may feel too big for you. We encourage you to do so anyway. Start by calling this to you. Do not be afraid: it will not happen all at once. It will be like everything else in your life: step by step, you will grow, you will change, you will transform, and you will feel strong and grounded in yourself — in your true self, as you amplify that personal power and that state of self-love, self-acceptance, self-worth, self-trust, that you have within you. It is already there, you do not need to go outside yourself to look for it, you simply need to tap into what you already have.

And if you feel that you don't have any of those things — maybe some of them, but most of them not — know that there is a seed *of all those things within you, so no matter how bad you may feel about yourself today, no matter how bad you may feel about your life or your experience, you have the seeds within you. You have the seeds of self-love, the seeds of self-worth, the seeds of self-acceptance, the seeds of self-trust, the seeds of everything you need to fully step into your personal power and live a life of power for good.*

We are so glad that you have returned to receive this message because it is so, so, so, important for as many people as possible to hear this message and know that however you may feel right now, this is possible for you. It is possible for you today to choose power for good.

That is all.

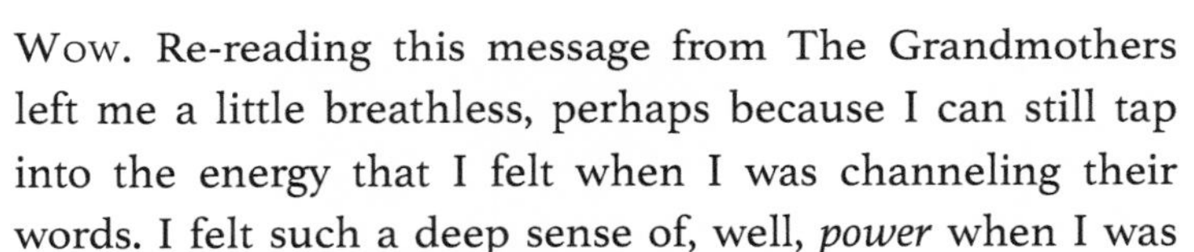

Wow. Re-reading this message from The Grandmothers left me a little breathless, perhaps because I can still tap into the energy that I felt when I was channeling their words. I felt such a deep sense of, well, *power* when I was receiving their message, and I feel that same sense of power whenever I re-read it.

There have been many points in my life where I have felt powerless: in particular, during a decade-long relationship where I felt trapped and unable to see a path forward and away from the person I was with. I had fallen into a deep sense of confluence with the other person — and not in a good sense of the word — where boundaries had been blurred and I was unable to find a way to extricate myself from the relationship and forge a life on my own. I had no sense of myself as an individual, but rather I viewed myself as an extension of the other person.

It was terrible. I felt like there was no way out. I felt stuck, with no hope of freedom.

I'm sure that many other people have experienced a version of this at some point in their lives: whether they've felt stuck in a soul-crushing job, or they've been in an abusive relationship, or they've made a series of decisions that have led them to feel stuck in life. It can be tempting to play the victim and to blame others for our situation: our overbearing boss, our narcissistic partner, or the difficulties of life. But the moment we stop pointing the finger at some external factor and turn it towards ourselves is the moment we can let go of blame and take responsibility for our lives.

They say that when we point a finger at someone else, we have the other three fingers pointing back at ourselves. Try it. You'll see what I mean. Don't get me wrong: I'm not saying we need to *blame* ourselves. I'm also not saying that we need to punish ourselves for our decisions in life. I'm simply saying that we need to *let go of blame* and *take responsibility* for our decisions — for the decisions we've made in the past and for the decisions we will make from this point forward. This is an incredibly powerful and life-changing shift in perspective.

And so, I encourage you to take the oath of The Grandmothers:

> *I choose power for the good. I choose to step into my personal power; I am ready, willing, and able to step into my personal power and to live a life where I am grounded in my personal power, which I choose to use for the good.*

Use whatever formality you choose: you can put your hand on your heart as you say the words, for example. Or simply say the words out loud. When we speak our intentions aloud, it's like casting a magical spell: we're giving our words power and we're sending our intention out to the universe. It may seem like a simple thing to do, but it's a ritual that holds great power and can plant seeds that will shift our path forward and change our future.

How about you? How do you feel about this personal

power stuff? Do you feel powerful or powerless in your life? Have you ever felt like you were a victim of your circumstances? Have you ever felt that bad things just happened to you, and that you were powerless to do anything about them?

How might it feel to flip all this on its head and step into your own power? How do you feel about taking the oath of The Grandmothers? Have you done it yet? You can do it right now. You don't need to make it into a special ceremony, though you can if you like. You can always take the oath now, in this moment, simply and without ceremony — and then do it once again in a special place.

If you choose *not* to take the oath of The Grandmothers — what's stopping you? Are you afraid of something? Why does it not feel right to you?

If you like the idea of taking an oath of personal power, and for whatever reason you don't resonate with the exact wording that The Grandmothers used, know that you can change the oath to whatever wording sounds and feels better to you.

14

THE THREE WITCHES

In the days leading up to Samhain, the 31st of October, I went to Avebury once again. It is said that both Samhain and Beltane — or May Day — are times when the veil is thin between realms. It's the time of year when physical reality meets spiritual reality, and the seen meets the unseen. It seemed like the perfect time to visit my favorite part of the world and to see if I could collect some new tree stories. I had intentionally visited Avebury on Samhain the previous year, and I was looking forward to returning.

After arriving, I headed straight to the little wood up at Windmill Hill. It was mid-autumn, and the earth was covered with a light carpet of fallen leaves that crunched as I walked through them and rustled as I shuffled my feet. The golden and russet tones of the leaves contrasted beautifully with the green of the evergreen trees and the ivy that snaked up the trunks of some of them.

It was a chilly day, and I was bundled up with many layers. My fleece-lined winter walking trousers kept my legs warm, and I had a number of layers on top, with more in my backpack in case I got cold. I knew that I often spent quiet time in this little wood, so I always carried extra bits of clothing for warmth, as my body temperature often dropped quickly when I sat in stillness in the outdoors.

I began to walk toward the multi-trunked sycamore that I usually visited with upon first arriving in the wood — the Windmill Hill Sycamore — but I stopped before I reached it. My eye was instantly drawn to a group of three small trees that stood together, forming a triangle between them. I had never noticed these young trees before, so it was odd that they caught my attention so suddenly. By now, I knew what this meant (a story was coming!), and I settled down against the trunk of one of them, curious about what was to come. Who were these trees? Why had I never noticed them before? They immediately answered my silent questions.

~

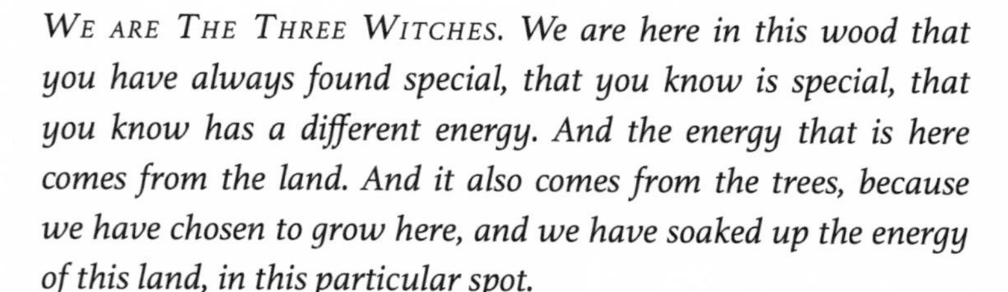

We are The Three Witches. We are here in this wood that you have always found special, that you know is special, that you know has a different energy. And the energy that is here comes from the land. And it also comes from the trees, because we have chosen to grow here, and we have soaked up the energy of this land, in this particular spot.

We are The Three Witches. We call ourselves that because we are here to teach witchy stuff.

It is not a coincidence that we had never caught your attention before. And now so close to the day of Samhain is when your eye was drawn to us — the second you stepped into this wood, in fact. We call ourselves The Three Witches not because we are here to help with witchcraft, or to teach you spells. We are not here to tell you a story of magic, at least not magic in the sense that you may be thinking. It is a different kind of witchy stuff that we are here to talk about.

You have become interested lately in the stories of ancient priestess-hood, of ancient feminine spiritual empowerment, and this is the energy that we embody, the three of us. We are here to tell a tale that will hopefully help any women reading this story to step into their soft power, or to at least take a step towards their soft power. And to any men who may be reading this, we encourage you to welcome the women in your lives as they step into this soft power, and we encourage you to step into it yourselves.

It is different, it is new, it will feel new, but it does not have to be scary, because not all that is new is scary. Not all that is new is meant to be feared. And any of you reading this that have any other gender, no matter what you identify yourself as; know that this is the way of the future. Listen up.

The old ways are coming back in a new way.

We know that sounds a bit like a riddle. It sounds like: what does that mean? But, the old ways of women fully stepping into their power in a soft, feminine, way, in a grounded way, in a witchy way, is coming back but in a modern form. This is Divine feminine power, this is power meant to heal, to help, to make a positive difference in the world. This is light power, and we do not mean light in the sense of "not strong": we mean it in the sense of white light — of bright, luminous power. This is what we mean.

And we encourage you to open your mind to what this might look like, to what this might feel *like. And this is something that the trees can help with: if you are ever out walking on a trail, walking in the woods, walking in a park and you sense a tree with witchy energy, witchy power, witchiness, approach it. You will know when you feel it. Go up to that tree and connect however you choose. You can sit against the trunk. You can sit and touch the bark. You can stand and do whatever you like. You can make contact with that tree and ask the tree to help you connect with your own Divine feminine power.*

And if you do not identify as a woman, ask that tree to help you see this power in women, to help the women in your life step into this power. And if you do not identify as a woman, ask that tree to help you *step into your own Divine feminine power, because everyone can have both Divine feminine power and Divine masculine power within themselves. This is the way of the future, this is the natural flow of events, this is the natural course of change. It has been long in coming and it is starting to happen. The time is now, and we encourage you all to embrace this. This is not women stepping into the strong, masculine, power. This is not that. This is not what you may think of power — it is very soft and grounded and flowy. It is very different. It will feel new, it will seem new, but it is old, old, old, and yet it is new in a way — it has evolved since the old days.*

And we are here, we The Three Witches, to remind you of this. We are here to remind you. We are here to encourage you to step into this energy, for it is delicious. It is the energy of the magical old crone, it is the energy of the magical maiden, it is the energy of the magical mother. It is the energy of that soft, beautiful, Divine, feminine power.

And if you have not yet experienced it, then perhaps you have seen it in someone else. Perhaps you have seen it in some woman that you find to be magnetic for some reason or another. That is the energy that we speak of. It is lovely, is it not? We do enjoy this energy, and we do enjoy seeing women stepping into this energy. The more women who embrace this soft, feminine, power, the more women who will be helping to bring life to the world. This is beauty. This is love energy. This is Divine. We will say it once more: it is delicious energy and we hope that you enjoy your journey as you discover it and perhaps step into it.

Thank you for coming to us, thank you for seeing us today, thank you for collecting our story, and thank you for beginning to step into your own Divine feminine power. We welcome you on this journey; we are delighted that you have read our story.

Thank you, thank you, thank you. This is all for today.

It makes me laugh every time I re-read the message from The Three Witches and their mission to teach "witchy stuff." It sounds so informal, and yet their story is so profound. I do believe in a time, way back in history, before the Common Era, when people lived with a sense of Divine power: of balanced masculine and feminine power. When men and women were equal, and one gender did not dominate over the other.

For the past two thousand years or so, we've lived in an era of masculine power, and it makes sense to me that humanity would swing back into balance at some point. When increasing numbers of people begin to embrace their soft, feminine power, this will help shift the balance of power into harmony once again. In fact, there has been increasing interest in the concept of Divine feminine energy, and I think it's important to point out here that this energy is not linked specifically to the energy of women, but rather to the feminine energy that exists within us all.

Feminine energy is often associated with intuition, nurturing, gentleness, creativity, and love. Masculine energy is often associated with logic, focus, analysis, and practical decision making. Feminine energy comes from the heart; masculine energy comes from the head. Feminine energy is being; masculine energy is doing. Ideally, we would want to have a balance of both of these energies, allowing us to live in a harmonious manner. And we would ideally want our governments, politicians, and law makers to function in an equally harmonious way. Unfortunately, this has rarely been the case for the past couple of millennia.

I think it's a good time to point out that "feminine" and "masculine" are terrible ways of expressing these concepts, mostly because these energies exist within us all, male, female, or nonbinary. But because these are the terms that are commonly used in today's society, I've employed them here. Feel free to use whatever language you prefer to describe these concepts. The important thing here is that we are all capable of harnessing these two main types of energy — being and doing, soft and firm, gentle and strong — and ideally we want to find a way to live with a balance of these in our lives.

That's why the messages from The Grandmothers and from The Three Witches are so important: when we're feeling powerless and dissatisfied with the current state of our world, we need to do what we can on an individual level to step into our own personal power and shift the state of things.

There's a lot that can be done on a personal level to step into our own power, and we can start by following the guidance and the wisdom of the trees in these last two chapters. The more we do at an individual level, the sooner things will begin to shift. We can already see changes happening in the world, and soon we'll reach a tipping point where we topple over into a sense of harmony and balance. At least, that's what I hope is in store for us.

I choose to believe in a better future for this world. I know this is possible, and I prefer to work toward it through my own personal development and by stepping into my soft power. You will know what's right for you.

~

AND WHAT ABOUT YOU? How do you feel about this Divine feminine power? Is it something that you resonate with? Is it something that you're willing to accept into your life? Are you willing to tap into this energy, and to help others in your life cultivate this? What terms do you prefer to express this "feminine" and "masculine" energy?

Do you believe in the power that you have as an individual to help change the world? If not, what would you need to believe in order to truly feel the power you have inside you to change things, even on a small scale?

15

SACRED SPRINGS SYCAMORE

One of my favorite places in Wiltshire is a sacred spring. On the OS Map, it's nothing more than some blue lines and a small patch of green woodland, but in reality, it's a place of deeply special energy. It's like a little bubble outside of time and space that you only really experience after climbing over the fence — the old stile is long gone — and crossing the large stepping stones that span the river, which is dry during the summer months, and gently flowing during the winter. Once there, the sounds from the nearby road seem to be muffled, and it's possible to enter a state of deep calm and peace.

To the right of the stepping stones, and just beyond them, a willow tree dominates the scene, with its trunk bowing down, forming curves that arch across the flowing water that pours from the spring during the wet months of winter. Its branches are adorned with multicolored ribbons and cloths — some fresh, some faded. Offerings are often left at its base. It is a wishing tree.

Its form is mimicked in an archway made of vines that stands to the left of the stepping stones. If you walk through this arch, which is also decked out in colored ribbons, a little path leads you up and to the left onto a little hill, where a large sycamore stands. It's a strange little grove littered with torn sheets of plastic, which I can only assume might have been used by people to camp up on the little hillside. Unfortunately, if this is the case, the campers did not feel the need to carry out their rubbish, and the large sheets of plastic stick out like a sore thumb in the otherwise pristine little wood. On one of my previous visits to the springs, this sycamore had let me know that he had a story to tell. This was on a cold wintry afternoon early in the year, when I had settled down against its wide trunk to have my lunch. After my meal, I warmed up with some hot tea from my flask, and I resolved to return at a later date to receive its story, perhaps when it was warmer and more comfortable to be sitting still for a time.

Despite returning to the spring several times after that visit, even during the warmer months, it wasn't until the days before Samhain that I actually sat down to collect the tree's story. The air was once again chilled, as we were deep into autumn, and I climbed up the little hill and walked a circle around the sycamore before settling in next to it. From my viewpoint up atop the little hill, I could see the wishing willow down below, and the fields beyond. As always, I was alone at the site. I knew that other people visited the spring, as there were always new ribbons whenever I visited, but I never saw anyone else when I was there. I sat in silence for several minutes, relishing the peace and tranquility of the site, before pulling out my phone to record the story. The sycamore spoke:

It is very important that you allowed yourself some time to

slow down before recording my story. It is important that you allowed yourself to sit against my trunk and soak up some of the energy of the place, for this is a special place, and you know it. You can feel it as soon as you come over the little fence and cross the river. Even when the river is dry, you feel a sense of crossing into another realm — which you are not exactly doing, but you are *crossing into a very special place: a place of the elementals. And you know this because it was told to you, but you would have sensed that energy anyway, even if you had come without knowing. When you have brought friends here, they have sensed it. All the people that come here feel something special, even if they don't understand it. But very few people walk up to this little hill, into this little wood, where we are, where I am situated.*

From here you have a view of the fields beyond, of the hill, the sun in the sky. You are surrounded by green, and you have the spring down below — that is where the center of the energy is, with the willow tree down below — and I suspect that tree will have a story for you, too. What I am here to tell you is to pay attention to these spots, to allow yourself to return as many times as you feel drawn to.

But I encourage you to spend time here. Not just five minutes, ten minutes: come, look around, leave. You can sit, you can have a cup of tea from your flask, you can have lunch, and you can sit and close your eyes and soak up the energy of this place and open yourself up to connect with the other beings that reside here. Just because you cannot see them, does not mean that they are not here. Some people can see them, as you know, but whether you can or you can't, it does not matter. You may want to ask permission to come into their special place, you might want to ask permission to stay awhile. Do whatever feels right for you. But you know that they are here, and know that they are not to be feared, no matter what stories you may have heard about them.

Stay awhile and close your eyes and open yourself up to the magic of this land. Soak up the energy. Sit, get comfortable, lie down, but stay awhile. If it is cold, you might want to put on an extra layer of clothing, as your temperature can drop. But stay awhile. Stay awhile and open yourself up to the possibilities of places like this, of connecting with the elementals, of connecting with the Nature spirits. Of connecting with the plant spirits, the tree spirits, the green spirits, the Green Man, the Green Lady, Mother Nature, Earth. It is especially easy to access these energies in a place like this, and it is particularly easy at this time of the year. If you are seeking to have a deeper connection with these types of spirits and energies, now would be a good time to come, now, or in May — or any time of the year, there is no bad time to come — to make a connection, to express your interest in communicating with them and developing a relationship with them, and to help them by caring for the land.

There are things that everyone can do. The first that comes to mind is recycling, but that is the norm now. That has been the norm for years and years, but think about how you can conserve energy — resources — this is how you help the planet, this is how you help Nature, by leaving a lighter footprint, by being more respectful if you are drawn to Nature. If you are drawn to the earth, if you are drawn to walking, to being outdoors, why would you not want to care for the planet, to care for the earth, to love it, to respect it? You may find that the more time you spend outdoors, the more than you will want to do: to care for the planet and care for the gifts that Mother Earth gives us. For she is here — she is everywhere, but her spirit is especially strong here.

So, I encourage you to come, come to places like this. Return as often as you feel drawn to. And I encourage you to change your life and change your habits. Change your way of thinking, change your actions, so we can care for this land, this land that gives you so much.

That is all. Thank you.

THE SACRED SPRINGS Sycamore was the first tree to talk about the importance of being kind to the planet — not just in the sense of watching where we tread, but in leaving a lighter footprint in terms of the natural resources that we use and how we treat our waste. He would not be the last tree with a message of this sort. It made sense that the trees would be concerned about how humanity is treating our natural resources: for years we have disrespected the Earth, taking what we want with no regard for the sustainability of our actions. It's time for more of us to take different actions that will lead to more sustainable living.

I loved that the trees were beginning to provide not just spiritual advice, but also practical advice on how to be kind to our planet. Our inner work must be balanced with our outer work — as we work on our personal development on a spiritual level, we must work on it on a practical level. It makes no sense to do things only halfway.

And while I sense that I may be preaching to the converted — most people who have a love for Nature or who are drawn to read a book of this sort will probably already be living an eco-friendly or sustainably minded life — there's always more we can do. There's always a little something more or something different that we can do to improve the way we treat this planet.

WHAT ABOUT YOU? How can you change your life to show more respect for our Earth? What habits can you change?

What things can you do differently? What actions can you take — big or small — to help the planet?

Are there any sacred springs in your area? This is not the first sacred spring that I've mentioned in this book, and I have found them to be places of very special energy. If you're not aware of any sacred springs near you, go online and search for one. You might be surprised to discover that there are several that you can visit.

16

WHITE ROAD OAK

I had been to Savernake Forest once before, and I felt drawn to return to it in the days before Samhain. I suspected that some of its ancient trees might have some stories for me, and I was not wrong. Savernake Forest is a Special Site of Scientific Interest located near the market town of Marlborough, just down the road from Avebury. This 2,750 acre (1,112 hectares) forest is privately owned by the Earl of Cardigan, his son Viscount Savernake, and his family Trustees. It is managed by the Forestry Commission.

Savernake Forest is full of ancient trees — in fact, it is believed to hold the highest concentration of veteran trees in all of Europe. This forest, made up of both native and non-native trees, is crisscrossed with tracks and footpaths, with some of the primary roads and tracks coming together in the very center of the forest at a place called Eight Walks. Savernake Forest is bisected by Capability Brown's Grand Avenue, a beech-lined private drive from the late 1790's that stretches almost four miles (6.5 km) long.

On the day that I returned to Savernake, just before

Samhain, it was a crisp autumn day, and the paths around the car park were full of dog walkers. I hurried to get out of the more transited areas, but it would be some time before I got far enough away to escape them. Shortly after parking my car, I took a photograph of the map of ancient trees that stood in the car park, and I had a loose plan of trying to find some of them. It seemed easier to organize my day in that way than to aimlessly wander the huge forest, wondering if I might come across one of the ancient trees.

One of the first giant trees that I came across was the White Road Oak. It immediately caught my eye, and I climbed up the bank and off the main path as I approached it, walking a full circle around its giant trunk before settling down against it. Its trunk was wide and gnarled, supporting its broad canopy above. I felt very exposed, as there was nothing to hide me from the main path, and people were walking all around. White Road Oak was situated right at a crossroads of two major paths and was still very near the car park.

I knew the oak had a story for me, but I was reluctant to pull out my phone and start recording. Dog walkers kept coming down the path, and at one point a large group of walkers went past with a guide. Fortunately, they didn't approach the tree, nor did they pause for long before hurrying off down the track. The White Road Oak seemed more than a little amused by my fears, urging me at one point to "get on with it!"

I knew I was being silly: after all, who cared what I was doing? What did it matter if people saw me talking into my phone, recording the tree's message? They probably wouldn't get close enough to know what I was doing and would think I was talking on my phone... in any case, I was about to make my tree channeling very public with the publishing of this book. It's not like I would be keeping my conversations with trees a secret. And yet, I waited for things to quiet down on this busy corner of the forest before I pulled out my phone to record this oak's story.

~

THE REASON *I told you to get on with it earlier is because you need to get over yourself when it comes to receiving these stories. Who cares what people think? As you can see, people don't care, people just barely look at us. You have just watched a group of about twenty people who have clearly come to this forest to see the ancient trees that live here, and they walked by, paused for a moment, and continued on. The guide did not encourage them to connect with me, to touch me, to spend some time in my presence, to feel my energy, nothing. It was just: "oh look at that tree, this is a big oak," and then they moved on. And they will do the same with all of the other trees they visit: today, tomorrow, and quite possibly always.*

It is fine to come and look at trees. Obviously, we are not offended by this. It is better than nothing: it is better than not *coming to look at trees. But we urge you to* connect *more with the trees. We are ancient, and I am hundreds of years old. I have been here for years and years and years, for generations of you humans.*

Please stop a while underneath our branches. Stop, rest, feel, experience. There are many people here who do not even stray from their path to come and look at me. You have just seen a dog walker pass by, glance over her shoulder because she saw you, and she must have seen me. I am much bigger than you are! But did she divert from her track, her path, to come and look at me? No, because she is just walking her dogs.

And this is fine, this is okay. We trees are pleased any time anyone comes to walk amongst us, whether it is to walk your dogs, or for a morning run, or for whatever. This is all fine and good.

But, if you are the kind of person who wishes to deepen your relationship with Nature, and who wishes to deepen your relationship with the trees, and the plants and all of the green things, then we urge you to slow down. Don't walk so fast; don't move so fast, just slow down. *And spend more time, walk more slowly, linger longer, and experience with all your senses: your sight, your smell. Do you even* smell *the forest? Pick up the leaves now that it is autumn, pick up the leaves from the forest floor, and smell them. Smell an old rotted log. Smell the green fluffy moss. Smell the trunk of a tree. Smell the air.*

When you go to the woods, are you really experiencing it with all your senses? This is another way that you can better connect with the woods, with Nature, with the green things. And we encourage you to do this. There are so many delicious smells. The soil: just kneel down and press your nose to the earth and smell — you might feel silly doing it, but that's okay, no one will care. They might look at you funny, but who cares?

And for those of you who have children: we would encourage you — I would encourage you — to see if your children would play in this way: to smell the forest, to touch the forest, to connect in different ways with their senses. It is wonderful to see children walking in the woods, but if you can encourage them to connect with us at a deeper *level, that is even better. Children are the future of this world, and the more connected they are to Nature the better it will be for this Earth, the better for this planet, the better for you, the better for me, the better for everyone who lives here. So bring them outdoors, bring them out dog walking, bring them walking, bring them in the woods, and if you can encourage them to connect at a deeper level, encourage them to touch, feel, smell — even taste if you are out when there are berries that are edible. Teach them to forage, and learn to forage yourself.*

Connect, connect, connect at a deeper level, and encourage your children to do the same. Encourage your nephews, your nieces, your grandchildren. You may be surprised to see how willing some children are to make these deeper connections, and you can make it play, you can turn it into play: you can make a checklist of different kinds of trees to find. Different kinds of things to smell, things to touch, things to feel, things to experience.

And ask them how they feel as they connect with each tree: ask them if each tree feels differently, or if they feel the same, or what they feel or how they feel. Ask them if they can sense the personality of the tree. They might think you are silly, or they might not, you never know. Make a game with it. Take your children out into the woods and see if you can turn this deeper connection into play. This is very important for the future. And we encourage you to have fun with it. If you do not have children in your life, we would encourage you to play yourself, to play with your senses in the woods. Slow down and have fun.

That is all.

THE FIRST TIME I had ever really focused on the scent of the woods was in January on the forest bathing Meetup that I attended, and yet I had seemingly forgotten to concentrate on using that sense in Nature throughout the year. Granted, the colder it is, the harder it is to smell the fragrances of the forest. But it's perfectly possible to get closer to the elements of the forest and do as the White Road Oak suggests: pick up the autumn leaves that carpet the woodland floor and smell them, bend down to get closer to a decaying log and smell it, pick up a tuft of green moss and sniff it. It's even easier to stand or sit next to a tree, turn to its trunk, and inhale deeply. And the air — what does it smell like? There may be a farmer burning leaves on their property, or the smell of a flowering elder tree nearby. Nature has so many smells!

I was grateful for the words of the oak in reminding us of the importance of not just connecting with Nature ourselves, but also encouraging future generations to do the same. Children or teenagers can try most — if not all — of the experiences recommended in this book by the trees. Though I went on this journey on my own, venturing out alone into the woods to connect with the trees and to collect their stories, there's no reason why you can't participate in these experiences with your children, your partner, your friends, or other family members.

The more we encourage others to connect more deeply with Nature, the sooner things will shift on this planet toward a more respectful treatment of the Earth. It's harder to disrespect someone or something when you know them deeply. That's why I occasionally take groups out on walks through the woods — to help encourage people to get outdoors and connect with Nature. Most of the walks I do are simply a stroll through the forest, while others have been more of a deeper woodland experience — including meditation and energy work in the woods.

What about you? Do you ever take time to focus on the smells of the forest? Do you ever pick up the damp fallen leaves or a tuft of moss? Have you ever bent down to smell a rotting stump? Far from being unpleasant, I find these forest fragrances to be earthy, woodsy.

What can you do to encourage other people in your life — especially children — to connect more deeply with Nature? This could be as simple as inviting a friend on a walk in the woods with you, with no particular agenda. Or you could invite a friend to try some of these activities with you. You could also go online and look for guided walks in your area — or you could also check my website to see if I'm offering any upcoming walks. Also look for outdoors courses, on topics such as foraging, plant identification, or forest bathing. There is so much that we can do to experience Nature in new and different ways.

17

SAVERNAKE BEECH

I felt such a strong connection to the trees as I walked through Savernake Forest. I wasn't sure if it was the energy of Samhain or the thinning of the veil, but I felt more open to receive the trees' stories than I ever had before. I continued down the smaller footpaths, trying to get as far away from the car park as possible, which I hoped would lead me to the quieter trails. I was attempting to avoid all the dog walkers who were out so I could tune in to the energy of the trees and possibly continue to collect more stories.

Walking down one of the smaller trails, I soon came across a giant beech tree that I recognized from my first visit several months prior. It was autumn, though, and not spring, so it looked very different. A colony of mushrooms was flourishing at the base of its trunk. It wasn't until I walked all around the tree and sat down on its far side, away from the trail, that I realized I had been there before, sitting in this exact place.

The wide trunk of the old beech was carpeted with lush green moss at its base. The earth around it was covered with a layer of russet leaves. A holly tree stood nearby, and all around were young evergreen trees, making the woods feel bright and verdant, despite the fact that we were deep into autumn.

I settled in, enjoying the apparent peace of the place. I was still fairly close to the car park, but this smaller path was less traveled, and there were few people walking by. The tree was big enough to shield me from the path, and I was sitting on the far side of the tree, away from the trail, which made me feel more comfortable about channeling the tree's story. It felt good to visit the tree a second time, in another season when it looked different. The beech spoke:

THANK you for taking the time to stop.

My message for you is to encourage you to return to the same places throughout the seasons. If you find a special place that you like, such as this — which I know that you didn't like so much the first time you came, and perhaps you are not liking so much this time, but you are drawn here — then return to it. You were here in spring and you are now here in the fall — and it is a very different experience.

You recognized me as soon as you saw me, but as you walked up to my trunk you saw the fungus flourishing at the base of my roots. You did not see this the last time in the spring because it was not that time of the year for the fungus to come up — now *is the time.*

You can see that my leaves are different: most of them are still green on the branches, and there is also a beautiful reddish yellow carpet of fallen crunchy leaves at my base. And I would like to encourage you to visit the same sites at different times of the year because you will see different things, you will smell different things, you will feel different things, you will experience different things. And by seeing different things in the same places, in every season of the year, this will help you to connect with the cycle of the year, the wheel of the year, the turn of the seasons. Now, of course, you know that autumn is when the leaves fall, winter is when it is cold, spring is when the flowers come, summer is when it is warm, but it is so much more than that. There is so much more detail, there is so much more to experience in each season of the year, in each month of the year, everything is so different.

You can see the holly straight in front of you, she has got berries on her branches, and she did not have berries when you came here in the spring. The smells were different, the air was different. The air is so crisp and chill today that you have to wear gloves. You did not need gloves when you were here in the spring; that was a different experience. And so I encourage you to find these special places and visit them over and over, at least once in each season. And perhaps to write about your experiences: you can get a notebook and save a few pages for each spot, for each site. You see that robin on the holly branch — what other birds do you see? What sounds do you hear? What smells do you smell? What textures do you touch? What do you see? What is different about all the trees and the shrubs and plants? Are there fruits out? Are there flowers out?

Dedicate several pages to each site and each time you go, write down as much as you can about what you see and smell and experience. Because this is part of deepening your connection with Nature: it is returning to the same sites and observing and experiencing and feeling. How do you feel? You, for example, feel cold. The air has a crispness about it that makes it such a delicious time to visit the woods. The sky is blue and clear, and it is a perfect, perfect day to be outdoors. And as you sit, under my branches, an occasional leaf will fall on you, and this is part of the connecting. So, what I have for you is the task of recording your experiences in particular places as you visit them throughout the year. You might use small notebooks and have a separate notebook for each place. Do whatever feels right for you.

And if it feels like too much work, then just pick one place and set the intention: put it in your calendar and see if you can make it happen. Take it out to the same place over and over again — at least four times a year in the different seasons. See what you see, see what you smell, see what you feel, see what you hear, but linger. See if you can connect with one particular tree throughout the four seasons, see how that tree looks and smells and feels. See if that tree's energy shifts throughout the year. And just linger.

Spend your time and perhaps observe other people as well. Observe how they experience the spot throughout the different seasons: do they walk faster in the winter, do they linger less? Are they in a hurry just to get their dog walked and get back to the car? Observe how other people experience Nature in different seasons. Experience how you *experience Nature in the different seasons: how do you feel? Are you cold, did you not wear enough layers? Do you prefer one season to the other? Which is your favorite season? What is your order of preference for all four seasons? But linger. Linger.*

Do you hear the delicious rustling of leaves in the wind? I love that sound. You would not have heard that a minute ago or a few minutes ago before the breeze picked up. I love that sound because I can hear my leaves rustle and I can hear the leaves of other trees rustling as well, and I feel like it is a song that we create: a symphony, of rustling leaves in the breeze.

And so this is my task for you: return, return, return to the same site or same sites, throughout the seasons. And experience, and record your experiences, because you may forget.

I hope that you enjoy the symphony of the trees when the wind blows. I thank you. This is all.

~

THERE WERE several places in Nature that I had visited over and over throughout the course of the year: the wood at Windmill Hill, the grove of The Grandmothers, the stone circle at Avebury. I had come to this very forest twice, in very different seasons. And yet I had never taken the time to stop and record what I experienced in each season.

On a later visit to the Avebury area, I took my journal up to the little wood at Windmill Hill and brought it out to record my experience. I was surprised by all the little things I could sense: I could hear the cars on the road far off in the distance, which I had never noticed before. A small plane passed overhead. Crows and songbirds were out. The live firing on Salisbury Plain rumbled every so often in the distance, like thunder.

It smelled *cold*. I could smell the damp earth beneath me as I sat up against my favorite sycamore — the one from Chapter 4 — to write. As I looked around, I could see the other trees of the woodland, the fields beyond, and the Ridgeway far off in the distance to my right. There was a small track down below where I was sitting, bisecting the fields. All around me was a carpet of leaves that had almost fully decayed after the dampness of winter. The trees all around were bare, except for the ones which were draped with ivy.

That was my first step in recording the sights, smells, and sounds of one particular site. I could sense how it helped me to connect more deeply to the place: by writing this experience down, it made me more acutely aware of the details, and it also provided me with a record for comparison on future visits. I resolved to get a new, smaller journal that I could use just for this purpose.

~

WHAT ABOUT YOU? Are there certain places in Nature that you tend to visit several times throughout the year? Have you ever stopped to record your experiences, or to compare what it's like in the different seasons? How do you think it might deepen your connection to those places if you were to journal about what each experience is like? If you were to pick just one place to record your experiences and observations throughout the seasons, where would you go?

18

POINTING OAK

I continued exploring Savernake Forest, heading deeper into the woods, away from the bustling trails near the car park and toward the King Oak and the Queen Oak. I didn't know what they looked like, but they sounded important, and I sensed that either one or both of them might have a story for this book. But before I reached them, I began to receive the story of a different tree. The words came into my mind even before I saw the old oak, and I was instantly curious as to where the story was coming from. I wasn't even aware that I was near one of the ancient named trees that were dotted throughout this forest — not all of them were on my map.

It truly seemed like the power of Samhain was making everything easier on this day. Instead of me seeking out the trees, they were now coming to me...before I even knew they were there. I soon came around a bend on the path and saw the source of the story: an ancient oak with a long horizontal branch that appeared to be pointing at something.

Its ancient trunk was gnarled and twisted, and parts of it were covered with thick green moss. Above, its canopy was made up of a variety of colors: green, yellow, and russet. The earth at its base was covered by grasses and bracken.

The energy of this tree was strong, and his story was a passionate rant. His energy was so intense that it was not surprising his message reached me even before I was aware of his existence. He started by calling me out on something I had done — or rather, not done — just before seeing him, and I felt ashamed of my behavior. I consider myself a lover of Nature, of the Earth, of the environment. And yet I often avoid doing one simple thing that can help the planet when I'm out on my walks. This oak's message was a very passionate reminder of one very easy thing that we can all do to help our woodlands.

My name is Pointing Oak. You heard my message before you even saw me or knew that I was here. You were looking for a different tree — a pair of trees. And instead, you came across me first, and you heard me before you saw me, because this is such an important message.

As you were coming around the trail, making a right turn, you stepped on an old empty bottle, and it crunched loudly under your feet. You were surprised, you looked down, and you kept going. And then you realized what you had done, and you turned and went back and picked up the bottle, and this is what I would like people to know: you always carry a rubbish bag in your backpack and yet you do not always use it.

I would like to encourage all of you who want to create a deeper connection to Nature, a spiritual connection to Nature, or simply spend more time outdoors to always carry a bag with you. It could be a small rubbish bag, it could be a big one, you can carry a number of small ones, whatever is easy for you to carry around — and please, please, please pick up the rubbish, that you see as you walk through the forest. It is shocking the things that people leave behind.

You see the size of this forest: anyone who has come this deep into the forest — because you are quite far off the main trails and you are quite far away from the campsite and the car park — anyone who has come this deep into the forest is clearly someone who enjoys Nature, who enjoys being outdoors, who enjoys walking. Why then, would they leave their bottles, why would they leave their rubbish? We are shocked and disgusted and repulsed by the behavior of people that do this. It is a disrespect. It is a disrespect to Nature, it is a disrespect to the woods, it is a disrespect to all of the green things.

Plastic: we do not like it, we do not like it, we do not like it. Please help us to remove the plastic that some very disrespectful people leave behind. This is something that I feel very strongly about, and that is why I pointed out the fact that you needed to go back and pick up that bottle. This should not be optional. You have a bag, you know that you can pick things up, and if you do not currently carry a bag, then you start. It is very easy. It is very easy to do. You can carry the bag in your hand; you can hang it off your pack. You can do whatever you need to do, but please, please, please, I ask you to help clean the plastic out of the woodlands.

This sounds like a very simple thing, and it is. And perhaps once you start doing it you will think, "Ugh this is such a pain, I don't want to be carrying this trash around." But if you love Nature, if you love the outdoors, if you love us trees: please, please, help us. This is something that we cannot do. Only you can help pick up the rubbish that other people leave behind. This is a problem, it is unsightly, it is an energetic disturbance. Plastic does not belong here: if you like to carry it in, then you must *carry it out.*

We take offense when these things are left in our territory. We take offense when people have the interest to come to us and yet are so disrespectful that they leave these things behind.

Now, you may be thinking: perhaps people are not intentionally throwing their bottles behind, perhaps they have fallen out of their pack? Well then, I tell you: secure it on your packs or secure it inside of your pack. Put your bottles, your plastic, in a safe place in your pack, period. It is not that difficult. We see the things that you carry, we see all the different places that you have to carry your rubbish in and to carry your rubbish out. It is absolutely possible, it is absolutely doable.

You may sense my discontent, anger, irritation at this. This is something that I feel very strongly about, and this is something that we all feel strongly about, we trees — this is a great disrespect to the woodlands. It is a great disrespect not only to leave the plastic behind but to walk past it on the trail. It is so easy to step down and pick it up, and even if you don't have a bag with you, you can tuck it into your own pack.

*So, I urge you, please: when you step on a bottle and you hear that plastic crunch, when you walk past a piece of plastic, please pick it up and carry it out with you even when it is not yours...*especially *when it is not yours. And I urge you to please start carrying a special bag with you, a rubbish bag that you can fill with plastic and take out with you.*

Please, please, please, I urge you on behalf of all the trees: this is important. You may think that compared to the size of this forest, a bottle is such a small thing. It is not, it is not to us. So, if you would like to deepen your relationship with trees, with the woods, with Nature, you can start by helping to clean up because that is something that we cannot do; we can clean the air, but we cannot clean the plastic. We ask for your help in this task. It is of great importance to us.

This is all. Thank you.

~

THE MESSAGE of the Pointing Oak was another impassioned message about the environment and about respecting Nature. Like the oak, it baffles me that people are interested enough in Nature to want to venture deep into the woods, and yet they leave plastic bottles and food wrappers behind them. Maybe it's laziness; maybe it's carelessness. As the oak said, it's quite possible that people have tucked their rubbish into their backpacks, only to have it fall off as they walk. That's why we need to be mindful of where we store our trash and keep it safely inside our packs.

I always have a little rubbish bag in my backpack, though to be honest I rarely use it. There are certain trails or spots that I know to be full of litter — such as the little grove where The Grandmothers stand — and I will go to those places and collect trash, but I rarely pull out my bag as I walk to pick things up. Because I walk with poles, it's a bit cumbersome to carry a pole in each hand and also lug around a bag of trash. But I can, of course, walk perfectly fine without poles, and it's easy for me to fold them up and put them in my pack when I walk through an area that's littered with bottles or plastic.

This is about making a little extra effort. Picking up bottles will not ruin a beautiful day's walk. On the contrary: when I do pick up rubbish, it makes me feel better about taking action to clean up the trails and woodlands that I so cherish.

~

HOW ABOUT YOU? Do you carry a bag around with you

when you go out into Nature? Do you ever pick up trash that other people have left behind?

So often we adopt the attitude that it's not our rubbish, so it's not our responsibility — and yet it doesn't take much effort on our part to clean up the woods. Are you willing to help? If so, what are you willing to do?

19

SAVERNAKE QUEEN OAK

As I continued my search for the King and Queen, I passed by a young tree with a sign proclaiming that it was the Replacement King Oak. It was a completely unremarkable tree and had it not been for its sign, I would have walked by without noticing it. I later learned that it had been planted in the 1980s to replace the Original King Oak and that it is the progeny of the Savernake Cluster Oak. I was disappointed to see that it was such a young tree, as I had been hoping to see the ancient King Oak, and I paused to see if the Replacement King had a story for me. It did not, so I continued onward toward the Original Queen Oak, who was very easy to find as she was clearly marked on the OS Map. I was grateful to see that she was still alive.

Located just off to the side of the trail, surrounded by a carpet of bracken, the Original Queen Oak is but a remnant of her past greatness. Her trunk is split, and her canopy has long broken off. She's essentially an ancient, barely living stump with a few small branches. This is a common tactic of English oaks: to extend their lifespan, very old trees of

700-800 years old will shed their broad crown, greatly shortening their height. I imagine that this helps to conserve energy and resources, thus extending their time on this planet. It's actually a very smart strategy.

The Original Queen Oak is an ancient tree, and her future replacement has already been planted nearby. At first, I was saddened to see her in such bad shape, but my sadness soon faded as I felt her vibrant energy. She was so full of joy that it was impossible to mourn her decaying state, and I can feel myself tap into that sense of bubbly joy every time I re-read her words. I hope that you, too, can get a sense of her cheerful energy.

Do not mourn for me. Do not mourn for me. I am overjoyed to have spent the hundreds and hundreds of years that I have been in this forest. Look at me, you can see how old I am. And look at all the life there is on me: the ferns, the moss, all the living things on the forest floor below me, the fungus on my trunk, nestled amongst my old chunky bark. And look up and see what is left of my own life, tiny little branches. I am so old, and I am so pleased to have been standing here for so long. I am so pleased to have been given the recognition that I have been given: Original Queen Oak. You can see that my king has fallen and there is now a Replacement King Oak.

Everything has a cycle, everything has a lifespan, and mine is coming to an end. I have many years of life left in me, but not as many as I have lived. Now you heard my message, far back on the trail, even before you heard Pointing Oak's message.

My message, my story for you, is a story of joy because that is what I feel. That is what I feel having been here for so many hundreds of years: the joy of being a tree, the joy of being in this beautiful forest, surrounded by other trees, of other species, other oaks, chestnuts, surrounded by bracken, all the green things. Look at the beautiful blue sky that I have stretched my branches towards for hundreds of years. I feel such great joy to have been here on this Earth, in this place, in the form that I have taken of the majestic Queen Oak that I am. You know I have presence. You know I am beautiful, and you can imagine what I must have looked like a few decades before — perhaps even a hundred years ago.

And so that is what I want to speak to you about: find your joy.

If you want to connect more deeply with Nature, find your joy in Nature. Do you enjoy walking, do you enjoy running, do you enjoy cycling? What is it that you enjoy doing in Nature? Do you enjoy meditating in Nature? Do you enjoy just going to the park and having a cup of coffee or tea? Find your joy outdoors, find your joy with the trees, find your joy with all the living green things, find your joy and do it. Make it happen.

Make it happen on a regular basis: find your joy and do it. *Give yourself permission to do the joyful outdoor things, which bring you a deep sense of happiness and connection, not only to the green things but to yourself. Find your joy and feel it, really* feel *it. And, as I said, give yourself permission to have these experiences, because sometimes people feel guilty. They come to the woods and they think, "I should be doing something else, I should be doing some work, I should be doing something with the family, I should do be doing emails, I should be paying bills." What they are really saying is: "I should be doing practical things."*

Now, of course, you can bring your family to the woods if you like, but when you find your joy, perhaps it is being alone *in the woods, perhaps it is being alone in the park. Whatever your joy is, give yourself permission to do it and make it a* priority *because it is an important part of you and your experience on this Earth. It will help you to deepen your connection to yourself, it will help deepen your connection to your Higher Self, it will help you deepen your connection to Nature and all the green things, so you find your joy in Nature and you* do it: *free from guilt. Give yourself permission to do this.*

How many trees have talked to you about the importance of slowing down? And perhaps your joy in Nature will be slowing down in Nature? Perhaps your joy will be jogging through Nature, cycling through Nature? There are different times for different things, so do not get this confused with other things that other trees have told you: there is a time for being still in Nature, there is a time for being quiet in Nature, and there is a time for living your joy in Nature and sometimes those things coincide and sometimes they do not. This is important for you to know, this task, this suggestion, this call to action of finding your joy in Nature is different from what other trees have told you. So, please experiment: find your joy.

Now if I were to ask you: what is your joy in Nature, what is your joy in the outdoors? How do you feel joy in the outdoors? What are the first things that come to mind? Write that down and if you think: "oh, I don't know, I don't know, how do I know that? That's such a big thing." Try. Experiment. Try one thing. Did you feel joy? If not, try another thing. Did you feel joy? If not, try another thing and keep trying, keep experimenting, keep playing, until you find that thing that is your joy in Nature and make it happen on a regular basis and really, really, feel that joy. It is delicious, *is it not? Hmmm.*

I am nearing the end of what I have to say to you and I am so pleased to have been able to share my story with you, my message for you, my task for you. My life has been full of great joy in this forest, I am so pleased, so pleased with my life. And I hope that you experience the same joy outdoors, in Nature, with the green things. Find your joy and experience it. Thank you.

~

THE JOY that emanated from the Savernake Queen Oak was contagious. Whenever I re-read her words, I feel the sense of supreme joy that she expressed through her message. Her story is an important one: lest we take this work of connecting with Nature too seriously, the Queen Oak is here to remind us to find our joy — to get clear on the specific activities that we most enjoy participating in when we're out in Nature and to just do them.

I think a lot of us — myself included — can take our personal development too seriously. I spend a lot of time identifying my fears, blocks, and limiting beliefs and doing mindset work with myself to shift them. I journal, and I have an extensive morning routine where I do my inner work. I walk my thousand miles every year, and I carefully track my progress toward my goals. It's all very serious. And while I love every bit of this, it's not exactly the sense of pure joy that I experienced when I tapped into the message from the Queen Oak.

The energy that I felt when she was giving me her advice was very playful, and I know that I often forget to play when I'm out in Nature, which leads me to wonder: what does Nature play look like for me? My answer: it looks like walking straight through mud puddles rather than gingerly stepping around them; it looks like cracking the thin sheets of ice with the toe of my boot on winter puddles; it looks like searching for new geocaches in the woods. Silly things, nothing really important — but they do bring me joy.

And this is important: our connection with Nature — as well as our personal development work — needs to be joyful. We need to play. We need to find our joy and *do it.*

~

How about you? Have you found your joy in Nature? Is it walking, meditating, cycling...or something else? And if you *have* found your joy, do you actually make it a priority in your life? Do you do it on a regular basis? If not, what can you do to make it happen more often?

If you haven't found your joy in Nature, what types of outdoor activities are you drawn to doing? What new things do you feel like trying? How would you like to play in the outdoors?

20

WESTERN HEMLOCK

I was still deep in Savernake Forest, trying to find my way toward the King of Limbs, when I walked past a section of non-native forest. There was a different feeling in this part of the woods: it felt dead and lifeless, despite being filled with seemingly identical evergreen trees, all of them reaching straight up to the sky with perfectly straight trunks. You may remember from Chapter 1 how I feel about plantations of this type. I hurried through this commercial forest as I looked for the trail that would take me to King of Limbs.

The western hemlock, or *Tsuga heterophylla*, is an evergreen conifer and member of the pine family that is native to the west coast of North America, from Alaska in the north to Sonoma County, California in the south. It's also known as the western hemlock-spruce. It is commonly planted for timber and wood pulp in Britain, where it stands out in sharp contrast to the native woodland. Western hemlock is valued for its rapid growth, making it well suited for a commercial forest. It was first introduced to Britain in the 19th century and it is now one of the most common conifers found in Britain.

The reason these western hemlock forests always felt so dead and lifeless to me is because they are often very dark and still. These tall, straight, closely planted trees cast a very dense shade, meaning that few plants and wildlife can live beneath them. It's eerie, which is not exactly the sensation I'm looking for when I enter the woods on my own.

As I hurried through this commercial forest, one of the western hemlocks stopped me in my path with his story, and I reluctantly paused to receive it. I stepped off the main trail, which was so far away from the car park that I no longer worried about someone interrupting me as I channeled the tree's story, and approached the tree. It had been at least an hour since I had last crossed paths with another walker, and I felt very alone in the woods.

The particular hemlock that called to me was located just off the path, and I stepped right up to his trunk, putting my hands on his bark. I looked around at the sea of apparently identical trees around me. The ground was littered with broken branches, and most of the surrounding hemlocks had bare branches at the lower levels of their trunks, the greenery reserved for the upper boughs. Because the particular hemlock which had spoken to me was right near the trail, it was bare on the forest side and green on the trail side, with long branches that gracefully sloped down toward the path.

The words of this Western Hemlock were humbling, even more so than those of the Pointing Oak. As I mentioned earlier in Chapter 1 when I received the Lone Oak's story, I have never liked walking through commercial forests: I don't like the energy of them. Something just feels wrong about this type of woodland. The trees all look the same, planted in straight, unnatural lines.

And yet, as this hemlock reminded me: they are still trees, just like all the others that I clearly have more respect for. After hearing the hemlock's words, I felt like a tree racist. I had been thinking of certain trees as being more valuable than others, simply because they were native to this land. As someone who has lived in a number of different countries and has spent over half her life as an expat, I was ashamed of my thinking. These trees were immigrants, introduced by foresters, and they were no less valuable or worthy of respect than any of the other trees in the forest. In fact, they served a very specific purpose.

I HAVE SOMETHING TO SAY. We feel like we are looked down upon. We know that we are not native, we have been planted here. We are not native to this land, but we did not ask *to be put here. We are not like other native trees in this wood, which would be allowed to live their full lives until they fall on their own or are struck by lightning, or are felled only because they are a danger to someone who is perhaps walking down the trail. We are here because we will be felled for our timber. You have seen the stacks and stacks of our relatives, trees like us. This is Forestry Commission land. This is what we are here for.*

You may think us ugly: our bare trunks, little naked sticks stuck out of them like a skinny porcupine, just a bit of green on the upper top of the tree, and a wasteland down below. Broken branches, piles of needles, dry needles, and far off some baby hemlocks which add a bit of interest perhaps to the woods. We are not here for our beauty, we are not here because we belong here, we are not here because we are native. We are here because we have been planted, and we have a purpose. As long as you humans need timber, as long as you need wood for your furniture, as long as you need paper, as long as you need those things that are made of trees, we will be here, we will be planted. Not us exactly, but others like us. This is our future, this is our purpose. We are here to serve a purpose for your people.

We are very different from the other trees you have talked to. You have mostly been speaking to native British trees and we are not that, we know this. But, rather than feeling the disdain, the disrespect of people as they walk through us, as they walk through this part of the forest that is not made up of native trees, we would like to feel your respect. So, maybe we are not as beautiful as an old oak, or a holly, or a hawthorn, but we are providing a service. We are here to provide a service. We give you things that you use, and we give you things that you need, and we would like respect. And perhaps you can try to see the beauty, you can see the beauty in our service, you can see the beauty in our uniformity, you can see the beauty in the little baby trees that you find here and again underneath the taller trees, perhaps you can find the beauty in this non-native forest. It is not totally devoid of life: if you can hear a bird over there.

Another tree spoke to you earlier of the symphony of the leaves in the wind, and you can hear that now. We also contribute to the symphony. You can hear the rustling of our needles high above. Why then, can you not appreciate our beauty? You can. *It is a change of attitude, it is a change of belief, it is a change of perspective. We would like to feel respect as you and others walk through this non-native forest, this commercial forest. The rustling of our needles in the wind, softly, look at our branches up high against the blue sky, we can be so graceful as we softly wave our branches in the breeze.*

We are not ugly, we are trees, just like the native trees, and we are here to provide a service. Do not think that we would not prefer to live out a long life, as do the oaks, as do the yews. Do not think that. But this is our lot in life, this is who we are, this is what we are. This is our purpose in life, this is our path, and we have the same tree spirits as the other native trees that you have been speaking to. We are also individuals, although we may look the same to you, we ask that you please, please, look upon us with respect, look upon us as individuals, short-lived individuals, who will be providing a service to you and to other humans. We are here to serve.

And I hope that you will learn to appreciate us, to value us, to respect us. And when you walk through a commercial forest made up of non-native trees, see it as something different, not lesser-than, but different. Pay attention to attitude and how it changes as you walk through the rest of this commercial forest and other commercial forests in the future, we ask please that you do not see us as lesser than, but rather different. And that you see us as individuals and you see the service that we are here to provide for you because that is our role.

Thank you.

WHAT CAN I SAY? I think the Western Hemlock said it all, and he said it so perfectly. These non-native trees are here to provide a service for us. They are living beings, just like the native trees that I had been speaking with in every other chapter of this book. And yet, they did not have my respect.

My attitude has changed dramatically since I received this story, and I now look at forest plantations in a very different way. I pause and try to see the trees as individuals, not as carbon copies of each other, no matter how closely each tree resembles its neighbor. I stop to hear the birds that *are* there, for there is never total silence in a commercial forest.

I stop, and I take a moment to be grateful for their service.

The Western Hemlock was right: they are *not* ugly. They

are beautiful green beings. They are Nature. And they deserve our respect every bit as much as the native oaks, yews, and hollies do. Whenever I receive a parcel in the post, wrapped in a cardboard box, I think of the Western Hemlock. When I open a book and turn its pages, I remember his story. When I open a door, I think of his words.

This chapter was an eye-opener for me.

WHAT ABOUT YOU? How do you feel about commercial forests, as they compare to native woodland? Are you prejudiced against non-native trees? If you're not a fan of non-native evergreen forests, do you think the words of the Western Hemlock might help you to see them differently?

Do you have any forest plantations near you? Are there any that you could visit and experience for yourself? If you go to a commercial forest (one that has a public footpath running through it; I don't encourage you to trespass), pay attention to how it's different from native woodland in your area. Are there different sounds? Sights? Smells? Textures? Energies?

21

KING OF LIMBS

At long last, I reached the far end of Savernake Forest and came upon King of Limbs, an ancient oak that is said to be more than a thousand years old. It's possible that its position makes it a parish boundary tree. Though I didn't know it at the time, it's thought that the Radiohead album of the same title was named after this old oak.

King of Limbs was easy to recognize from the trail. A narrow path led off through the lush green bracken and made it easily accessible. The ancient tree had a sparse canopy that was suspended by three main trunks, and a number of broken branches lay on the ground next to the oak.

There was a strange energy in this area of the forest, though I had left the commercial plantation and was now in native woodland. As I mentioned in the previous chapter, I had finally escaped all the dog walkers, and it had been some time since I had crossed paths with another person. I felt very isolated and alone, yet it wasn't quite the peaceful sensation I had expected. Something felt...off, yet

I couldn't put my finger on it. I became hyper-aware of the energy around me in the forest. I was growing increasingly uncomfortable, and I was very aware of how alone I felt.

All that changed when I sat inside the hollow trunk of King of Limbs. As I approached the tree, I could see that his trunk was split open in the middle, with more than enough space for one person to sit comfortably inside. I took off my pack and crawled into the tree, setting my pack alongside me. I relaxed and tuned into the energy inside the old oak.

There was such magical energy inside the tree, it was almost like an energetic microclimate, and I settled in to see if he had a story for me. As I waited, I relished the lovely energy of the place. I forgot the uneasiness I had experienced just a few minutes prior. His energy was so beautiful that I even entertained the fantasy of camping out in the woods and setting up a sleeping bag within his trunk (I say "fantasy," because wild camping would not be permitted in this forest outside of the designated campsite, which is located near the car park). At first, I didn't think the old oak had a story to share, but eventually, he piped up with a message.

You were very pleased to see me and then when you came inside and sat down, you felt as though there was no story, that there was not going to be a story. My story is to tell you that there are some places like this where you feel a kind of bubble of energy. It could be in the belly of an old tree, like me, it could be a place like a sacred spring, or any of the special places where you have felt that you step inside a place and it is almost like you are cut off from the rest of the world, separate, almost as if you are in a different dimension. These are the places where you must sit awhile: just sit, you can do anything. You don't have to observe,

you don't have to experience, you don't have to be silent; you could look at things on your phone, you could read a book, you could listen to music.

It doesn't matter what you do, because when you go to these places you are there to receive energy. This could be healing energy, this could be vitalizing energy — it is the energy of that place that you are there to receive. And sometimes it is best if your mind is not active, so you may think: "oh those are the places where it is good to go and meditate, and focus on the energy, and be very serious" — but not necessarily. These are places where it is often good for you to do what you just did when you sat in here, which was to look at a map and plan your route back. These are places for you to read, places for you to keep your conscious mind engaged so that the energy can slip in and swirl around and do its job in your physical body. Of course, you can do whatever you choose. I am just here to tell you that this is one of those places: you feel it, you know it.

So, stay as long as you feel drawn to, whether it is one minute, or five minutes, half an hour, an hour, or longer. When you start to feel restless, then you know that it is time to leave because you have received what you were meant to receive. Do what you need to do to stay warm, to stay cool, depending on what time of the year it is: put on an extra layer of clothing, take off an extra layer, do what you need to do to be comfortable during the time that you will be in these special bubbles of energy.

Do what you need to do to keep your mind busy, and just allow yourself to soak up the energy, consciously or unconsciously, of these special bubble sites. There is really not much more that I can tell you about this: just be open to feeling those special places, and you know that you are there when you are drawn to a certain place and you sit down, and you feel like you are in a different space, most likely there is some kind of protection, or filter, between you and the rest of the world; you hear the leaves rustling in the trees but sounds really, really, far off. It doesn't sound like it is right next to you, that you are in that part of the woods. These are the places where you can receive great energy, and again, you do not need to do anything, you just need to be there.

So we encourage you to keep your mind busy when you go to these places, don't over think things, don't make it out to be more serious, or more spiritual, or more whatever than it is. It is just is what it is, it is just energy, and it flows — just doing its thing, no big deal. But I encourage you to sit a while in these places, and you will know how long. Thank you.

ONCE MORE, I was reminded of the bubble of energy. I kept coming across these sites as I researched this book, and the trees in each place confirmed my feeling that they were indeed special places. I found it interesting that he was encouraging us to keep our minds occupied so the energy could slip in and do its work. This was very similar to a tactic that my former spiritual teacher employed with the group, telling jokes and stories as he did his energetic work in the background, unbeknownst to us. As King of Limbs said, we often feel like we need to do serious, important things in these energy bubbles — such as meditate — when in reality, it doesn't really matter what we do. We could quiet our mind in meditation, or we could keep our mind busy by looking at a map or reading a book, allowing the energy to do its work in the background.

It was getting late, and I had to get back to Avebury for an appointment with Sara. I looked at my watch and saw that I had just barely enough time to make it. I was reluctant to leave the delicious energy of King of Limbs, but I knew that I could always return.

I stood up to leave the peaceful energy bubble of King of Limbs and as I stepped out of the energy bubble of his trunk, the deep sense of uneasiness returned, this time even stronger than before. I felt scared and I peeked around the other side of the old oak to see what was there. Of course, I could see nothing. Once more, I was sensing the unexpected energy of something I couldn't see with my eyes. I grabbed my pack and headed back toward the main path, looking all around me. I could see nothing — and no one — in any direction.

I pulled out my phone to consult the OS Maps app so I could find the fastest way back to the car park. King of Limbs was probably the furthest possible point in the forest from where my car was located, and I knew I had a long walk back, even if I went the most direct route. My phone battery, which had been at about 40% just before I stepped inside King of Limbs, immediately plunged to 0% and it died instantly. I had not had previous trouble with my phone battery, and it was not so cold outside for me to think that the temperature had something to do with it. This felt like a very clear sign that it was time for me to leave.

I would like to be able to say that I stuck around, welcoming whatever it was that was causing the strange energy and attempting to get to know it. That's not what I did. Instead, I took one last look around me and then I speed walked back to the trail, past the Western Hemlocks, and onward, not slowing until I reached Grand Avenue, where it was a straight walk almost all the way back to the car park.

Once I entered this more populated section of the forest, with walkers, cyclists, and even cars driving by, I relaxed and mulled over what I had just experienced. I had no explanation for what had happened to my phone — the battery had never done that before. I also had no explanation for the strange energy I had felt. Had some unseen being shown up? Why did it feel so dark and scary? Was it simply because I couldn't see what was there? I had no answers, and I hurried back down Grand Avenue toward my car as it was approaching sunset.

Upon reflecting on this experience, I've realized that this situation should not have been terribly surprising to me: as I mentioned in Chapter 1, oaks are said to be a doorway to the mysteries of this world, a boundary crossing between one place and the next. And here I was, experiencing just that.

I've also realized that I would like to return to King of Limbs and see if I feel something similar again — maybe not during Samhain, but perhaps during Beltane, when the veil is also thin, but the energy is lighter in feeling. I know that I need to get used to situations like this, and I'm very curious to see how the site feels during another time of the year, outside of the energy of Samhain.

HOW ABOUT YOU? Do you feel like you have to do something special or important when you sit in places that feel like an energy bubble? Or are you content to simply sit there and do whatever you feel like?

What do you think you would have done if you had felt the strange energy near the old oak? Would you have stuck around and investigated? Would you have tried to see what was there, or feel into its energy more? Would you have tried to make contact with it? Would you ever return to a place where you felt something so strange and uncomfortable?

22

THE FOUR KNIGHTS

The next day, on this same trip to Avebury just before Samhain, I returned to the little plantation at Windmill Hill. After spending some time in the wood, I approached a cluster of sycamores that I had spent some time within the past. Much like the first Windmill Hill sycamore I spoke with in Chapter 4, this was a cluster of four trees growing together.

As other groups of trees or multi-trunked trees have done in other chapters, it was one sycamore who spoke, as though he were the representative of them all. It seemed as though the energy of the group was flowing through all four of the trunks, and they were all in alignment with the message that came forward.

Their message was very timely for me, as I had received a soul code reading from Sara O'Dowd the evening before, and this very topic had come up in the session. With channeling, I sometimes find that something has to come into my awareness on a practical level before I can channel further information about it. It's as though I need to have information about something in my physical reality before

I can receive further details about it from my guides or from the plant spirits. In any case, it was perfect timing: it felt as though they were expanding on a concept that I had just recently learned about in the numerology session.

This message from the trees involves a concept that you may or may not believe in: reincarnation. As with any of the other concepts presented in this book, please take what you like and leave what you don't like. Keep what serves you and leave what doesn't.

We are The Four Knights. As you can see, we are four trees that have grown together in a cluster, and we are here to represent the multi-layered soul that we are and that all living beings are. Your soul has traveled through many lifetimes, and your soul has chosen to experience very specific things in each lifetime. Your soul has chosen specific challenges for each lifetime, and it has chosen specific things it would like to experience in each lifetime, in order to grow and evolve into the multi-layered soul that it strives to be. And this is why sometimes things are difficult, sometimes things are challenging: these are things that your soul has chosen to experience, to help your soul to grow.

Now, oftentimes, we see people getting caught up in their current lifetime, in their current struggles, in their current situations, while failing to see the bigger picture: the overarching theme of what they have chosen to learn and how they have chosen to grow. And oftentimes people fail to understand that they have chosen the situations that they are experiencing in this lifetime.

Now, one of the big challenges in life is to put your current lifetime, and personality, and challenges, a bit to the side so that you can integrate all of your lessons, all of your learnings, all of your richness of previous lifetimes and bring all of that into this current lifetime. This can be a challenge because it is so easy to get caught up in everyday life difficulties, in everyday life struggles, in everyday interactions with other people. But there is more to life than that, and the sooner you can bring in all of the gifts from your previous lifetimes, all the things you have learned from your previous lifetimes — the sooner that you can bring those lessons into your current life — the sooner you will begin to experience flow and ease and a sort of settling into this lifetime. This is something that you must remember from lifetime to lifetime to lifetime, and yet you forget.

Now, for us trees it is easier because we hold a deep connection to the land, a deep connection to the other trees: we always have a network, we always have access to experiences from previous lifetimes. It is not so easy for you humans, and yet it is possible, and it is doable, and you can do it. So we are here to suggest that you give it a try: we suggest that you bring these learnings from your previous lifetimes into this life. Now, the first step is becoming aware that this is a thing: that this is a possibility, and that this is something that you can do. The next step is to set the intention: to set the intention to the Universe that you are willing to do this work, that you are ready, willing, and able to bring all of the multi-layers of your previous lifetimes into this lifetime and that you are ready, willing, and able to integrate them and live from this place of soul being.

This is the best way to start this path. The more you open yourself up to this possibility, the easier it will be for this to happen. The more you ask for help from the beings around you, whether it is the Nature spirits, angels, whatever you choose to ask for help with, the easier it will be to integrate these parts of you, because these are all parts of you: these are all multi-layered parts of your being, even though you may feel that you currently do not have access to them.

So walk the land, meditate, slow down, do whatever it is that you need to do to connect with yourself, and when you do so, set the intention to connect with all the multilayered dimensions of yourself, of your soul, over all the years and years and years and millennia of lifetimes. We ask that you do this work, because the more people that do this work, the faster your society — the faster the energy — will evolve on this planet, and that will be a better place for you, and that will be a better place for us, and for all living beings, including the Earth.

Now more than ever it is easy to do this work. It is easy to walk this path. It starts by setting the intention, and because you are already aware of this, we ask that you give it a try.

That is all.

THE MESSAGE of The Four Knights is very much aligned with a channeled message that I received a couple of years ago from some spirit guides who called themselves Orion, who were the guides that brought me my energy healing and mindset-upgrading technique that I call Heart-centered Energy Work®. I remember feeling a great joy when that message came through, which is available to watch on my YouTube channel. It was almost a relief to hear that the more challenging things that I'd experienced in my life were situations that my soul had chosen to experience in this incarnation. It gave me a whole new perspective and also more of a sense of power over my life: rather than having had certain negative or difficult things happen *to* me, I had actually *chosen* to experience them, even if I didn't remember making that decision. Now, I know that this isn't how most people see life. But it's a theory or perspective that I've been familiar with for a couple of years now, and it honestly feels right *for me.* Plus, it feels much more empowering.

Part of the message that I had received in the soul code

numerology reading with Sara was about bringing forth the wisdom that I had accumulated in previous lifetimes into *this* lifetime, and I was so happy to hear that The Four Knights were echoing this message for me. It feels like something that's so difficult to do, and yet for the past year or so I've been starting to feel like I'm tapping into the knowledge of who I might have been in previous lifetimes.

I've felt increasingly drawn to read novels about herbal healers, for example. Every time I read a book that is set in history where the main character is a medicine woman or herbalist, it feels so familiar to me. And I feel a sense of longing, a sense of nostalgia — as if I wish I could go back to that. This has become a recurring theme for me in recent months, and it's led me to sign up for a number of courses this year that teach not only the foraging and use of plants for food and medicine but also how to work with the spirits of plants for healing. These are things that I'll be learning for the first time in this lifetime, but I feel as though these are things that I already knew from previous lifetimes. If only I could tap into those memories!

It appears as though I can — that we all can — and I have set the intention to do so, since The Four Knights indicated that setting the intention was the first step. I have intentionally opened up to the possibility, and I look forward to seeing what — if anything — I am able to remember. I wonder if practical learning and knowledge in this lifetime will activate some of those memories for me. I wouldn't be surprised if they did.

WHAT ABOUT YOU? Do you believe in the possibility of past lifetimes? If so, do you believe that you might possibly be able to access all that you learned in your previous lifetimes? Are you willing to set the intention to bring that knowledge and wisdom into this current lifetime?

How do you think it would change your life if you could remember all the wisdom that you have accrued throughout numerous lifetimes? Do you think it would lead you to make different decisions? How might it change the way you feel about things?

23

TWIN SYCAMORES

As I wandered around the Avebury stone circle, I headed toward a pair of trees that had reached out to me in June to tell me they were in this book. They were located in the southeastern quadrant, in an area of the stone circle that I rarely visited, as most of the old stones had been pulled down and destroyed in this section and there was not much left to see. It was now early November, less than a week after Samhain, and I felt that it was time to receive their story. I was very much aware that I was in debt to them, as they had expressed their interest in being a part of this project five months earlier.

I walked past the main part of the stones toward a part of the field where people rarely ventured. The stone circle had been mostly destroyed in this area of the quadrant, the individual stones pulled down and broken up to build the houses and barns of the village. I always felt a bit sad when I walked in this part of the field: so many of the stones were missing, and it was a somber reminder of what little importance the local farmers and villagers gave to this ancient sacred site in centuries past. There was just one fallen stone in this part of the quadrant, located far off in the field near a ring of trees just before the ditch that circled the four quadrants.

The twin sycamores stood at the very edge of the field, next to a fence that separated the grounds of the stone circle from Green Street, the quiet country lane that led to a few rural homes and a farm, where the asphalt ended and the byway continued all the way up to the Ridgeway National Trail at the top of the hill. The only cars that went down the road were those of local residents or delivery vehicles, and the only pedestrians were the few visitors that were exploring the stone circle.

It was a cold afternoon, and I pulled on my thick fleece gloves to keep my hands warm as I settled down against the trunk of the trees. The ground was carpeted with fallen leaves, and the ancient site was fairly quiet, as it tends to be in the colder months. The Samhain tourists were all gone, and only occasionally did I see people walking down the quiet country lane on the other side of the fence. It was easy for me to settle in and channel the story of the trees.

There is a time and there is a place for everything. And sometimes you will feel satisfied by the timing you experience in your life, and sometimes you will feel frustrated and feel dissatisfied. Sometimes you want things to happen, specific things at a specific time. Sometimes it is possible, often it is not. You must learn the delicate balance between wanting, setting goals, taking action, planning to do things, to make these things happen in your life, and balance that with trusting that everything will happen at the perfect time for you and that you will experience the perfect experiences that you have come here, and chosen to come here, to experience.

Sometimes these will be enjoyable, sometimes they will not. If you take advantage of these experiences, if you take advantage of all of these experiences, they can all be very useful in your growth. Oftentimes people fall into the victim trap of feeling sorry for themselves, and this does not serve you. So my lesson for you, my story for you, my message for you, is to pay more attention to the seasons. Every year it is more or less the same, every year you have more or less the same seasons, sometimes they start earlier and sometimes they start later. Sometimes one season is longer, another season is shorter. There are variations: it is not exactly the same, but you can expect winter, spring, summer and fall, every single year. There are cycles; these are things that you can expect. These are things that we can expect as trees.

Observe the changes, know that nothing lasts forever, and see if you can relax, and flow. Relax and flow through the seasons, relax and flow through the changes, relax and flow through the experiences of your life. Let go of worry, nothing lasts forever. Pay attention to the things that you want to experience and focus on those; know and trust that they will come when it is their season and it is their time. And the season for the changes, these things that you want to experience, may or may not be aligned with the timing that you wish for, and this is okay. Relax and flow into the changes. Focus on the changes that you want to experience and relax...do not be too — we do not want to say committed — do not be too stuck *on any one idea, because there may be something better for you, there may be something more satisfying for you to experience that you have not even yet conceived of. And it might be that by taking action toward the thing that you want, that a new thing opens up to you, in different timing, or in the same timing.*

Relax, and allow yourself to flow through the seasons of your life focusing on what you choose to experience and knowing that surprises may happen, surprises may come, unexpected things may occur, and this is all right. This is to be expected. This is to be relished. This is to be savored. Oftentimes people do not welcome surprises, and they are disappointed by them; they are frustrated by them because it is not what they expected, it is not what they wanted. Again, I tell you: relax and flow through the seasons of your life and open your arms to the unexpected experiences. Ask what you might learn from this experience, what you might learn from not having the experience that you wanted instead. And going into Nature, and sitting in Nature — not just walking but stopping and sitting — will help you to slow down and integrate the gifts of these experiences.

Allow yourself to slow down.

I know I am not the first tree to tell you this. You may find yourself hearing the same, or similar messages, from different trees, because we see that this is very much needed in your world. Flow, flow, flow — gently, not violently — your life does not need to be a river of rapids; it could be a gently flowing stream. And you may find flowing through your life as a gently flowing stream to be more satisfying, more manageable. Slow down and go out into Nature and observe the changing of the seasons.

It is fall now, and I have lost most of my leaves: there are some falling from my branches as you record this, as you sit here, receiving my message. The ground underneath my branches is carpeted with crispy leaves, some of them freshly fallen, some of them dried and brown. We are approaching winter, then spring, then summer, and it all begins again, it all continues. It is a cycle, as your life is a cycle, and the more you pay attention to the cycles in your life, the easier it will be to flow: to flow through the cycles of your life, and to flow through your experiences, and to appreciate each and every one, even the unexpected experiences.

This is all.

UGH. The concept of Divine timing is such a source of frustration for me. While I do believe, deep down, that things happen for a reason (usually because there's a lesson that we needed to learn), and that everything always falls into place at the perfect time, I tend to feel incredibly frustrated when things don't happen in the way and at the time that *I want them to happen.* I get impatient, annoyed, discouraged.

When I'm going through an experience like this — where I'm not getting what I want, when I want, how I want — it makes me feel stuck, like I'm taking two steps forward and falling one step back. Like I'm not taking the right actions or making the right decisions. Like I'm not *doing enough,* and yet when I look back over my life and see how things have flowed and changed, I can see the natural progression of things. Sure, it didn't happen as fast as I wanted, or in the way that I wanted it to, but it all happened in the end, and sometimes in a different way than I expected — a better way.

I've been self-employed since 1999, and my entrepreneurial journey has had two distinct phases so far: first, a hospitality business that I ran for ten years with a business partner, and then a coaching and consulting business that has had many iterations. I was a life coach, then a social media consultant, then a business coach. The last phase of this was business mindset coaching, where I worked with entrepreneurs to help them overcome their blocks to creating a successful business. I absolutely loved it.

Until I didn't. I started to become disenchanted with the online business world: I was so sick of the formulas and fake-feeling marketing tactics. It got worse and worse, until

I ended up essentially quitting that part of my business late last year. Why? To focus on my writing.

Now, when I look back on the last couple of years, it was clear that I wanted to dedicate my time to writing books. But yet I was still trying to fill my calendar with mindset clients, which of course left less time for actually writing. It wasn't until my business actually died down, to the point where I was once again struggling to find clients, that I realized what was going on: I was no longer energetically aligned with that business, and by making it hard for me to find clients, the universe was giving me the time and space to write, essentially forcing me to make my decision to let go of my mindset business and focus on my books.

Since I made that difficult decision, things have been in flow. I've focused on writing this book, and I've got other Nature-based books planned for the future. While I still love mindset work, and I do still see mindset clients, I'm no longer focused specifically on *business* mindset, and I only open up my calendar for client sessions every once in a while. Everything flowed into place, and everything now feels right. I feel like I'm on the right path again with my life. And yet, none of this happened in the way that I planned. It was frustrating and at times it felt awful, though I suspect that if I had just taken the advice of the Twin Sycamores to relax and flow, and to remain open and curious about what was going on for me, it would have been a whole lot easier.

WHAT ABOUT YOU? Do you believe in the concept of Divine timing? Are you good at relaxing and flowing through the ups and downs of life? If not, how do you think your life might be different if you did allow yourself to relax and flow? Might it make things easier?

When you look back over the years of your life, can you see how everything fell into place? Can you see how things that were difficult or painful actually taught you valuable life lessons?

24

THE SOMERSET FOUR

There is a little wood in Somerset, near Glastonbury, that I had wanted to visit for many months, ever since it was first mentioned to me by a friend. It's said to be a magical place, full of fey energy, but also very muddy, so it was better to visit in the drier months rather than in the winter. I knew it was getting late in the year, but I suspected that one or more of the trees in this woodland might have a story for me, so I decided to drive out to Somerset and risk sitting in the mud to receive a message. It hadn't rained in a few days, so I thought I might be in luck. I parked in the nearby village and walked toward the wood, which was located off the little road that wound around the village.

There was no one out on the trail that led to the woodland. It was a crisp, quiet day, and I was all alone as I entered the forest. It was November, and the trees were bare and wintry. I walked down the main trail that led straight through the woodland, looking all around me and trying to tap into the energy of the place and get a feel for it. I didn't immediately sense the specialness of the place, which was disappointing. I wondered if it was because it was winter, and things were dormant...or whether this simply wasn't the right place for me. Maybe I wasn't meant to visit here, after all? It was at that point that I realized I had heard so much about this woodland that I had built up high expectations for my visit.

I continued walking down the main path that led deeper into the woods, and it wasn't until I arrived at a little grove made up of three yews and one young oak that I felt it: this *was* a place of special energy. There were three small logs arranged in the clearing of the grove, and I sat for a few minutes on one of them before deciding to perform a simple ceremony. I thought it might give more of a sense of structure and importance to my visit, though in reality, I think it also served to help me relax and tune into the energy of the woodland. After I finished, I returned to the log and sat down once more, looking all around me, feeling into the place.

There was a slight breeze, and a broken tree creaked as it leaned against another, sounding like a squeaky door opening and closing. The two trees were just beyond the little grove where I was sitting. I got up at one point to see if I could determine exactly which trees were causing the noise. The creaking of the trees was slightly unnerving, like something from a horror film, and it was impossible to ignore. It was always in the background, the entire time I was in the woodland. Creaking, creaking. It was eerie, and I was hoping I wouldn't have an experience like the one I had near the King of Limbs. I was aware that I was all alone in the little wood.

I soon relaxed, and I felt drawn to connect with the four main trees of the grove, and I approached them in turn: first the oak, then one of the yews, then the other two yews. Once I made contact, I felt such an instant connection with them that it was almost as if they were human. I realized that my relationship with trees had deepened as a result of this work of collecting tree stories: I truly felt that I was meeting a living being with a distinct personality, rather than an inanimate object. I was seeing and feeling and interacting with the trees as individuals.

Be spontaneous.

Do whatever pops into your mind.

Do not be worried of what others might think, and do not be worried by what others may think of you: hugging a tree, or sitting against a tree, or however it is that you choose to engage with the trees. Really feel *what you need, feel what you need, feel into the experience of interacting with the trees. You just went up to the oak, in the middle of our triangle, and you hugged the oak because you felt drawn to do so. But you* really *hugged the oak — you felt like you were hugging a living being. It wasn't just the intellectual act of putting your arms around a tree: you felt it. In the same way that you felt it, other people can feel this too.*

You should know by now that each tree has a different personality, a different energy, a different way of being. Go to the trees that you are most drawn to and really, really, feel them, feel their energy. You did not intend to feel that tree's energy or have such a good hug of the tree when you went up to it; you felt drawn to hugging the tree and so you did. And this is what we encourage everyone to do. Do what you feel drawn to do, and linger, and relax, and give yourself permission to spend time engaging with the tree. To spend time feeling *into the tree, and sense what happens.*

When you went to the first yew, you felt that you needed to sit down with your back against its trunk and you felt that energy seep into your body from the tree, and you felt that you had to encourage yourself to relax, so you focused on relaxing all the different parts of your body. You closed your eyes and you gave yourself permission to relax and you felt that energy flowing into your body from the yew, and you felt it, and you felt it, until it was as if a tap had been turned off and you got the sense that it was enough, that it was time to move on and so you did.

And then you came to me, and you can sense the energy flowing into your back from my trunk. You will know when it is time to get up and leave, and if you do not, there is no matter; there is no prescribed length of time to engage with the trees. What we encourage you to do is to give yourself permission to relax, and to feel into each tree. Trust your intuition, trust your gut, when it tells you how *to engage with the tree, whether it is hugging it, or sitting up against it, or any of the other things that you have learned in these stories from the trees that you have already heard.*

Give yourself permission to relax and receive, relax and receive, for we have good things to give you. And if you stay too long or if you stay not enough time, that is okay. The more you do this, the easier it will get, the more you will trust yourself, and the more you will know. The important thing is to start. So the next time you are out in the woods, pay attention to what you feel drawn to do, and give yourself permission to just relax and receive; relax and receive and feel. *Feel what it is that you are receiving from the tree, feel what it is that you are giving the tree. It is a symbiotic relationship, you might call it: relax and connect, relax and connect.*

Enjoy, and know that when you go out into Nature and you receive from the trees, and you receive from the spirits of the land, know that you will need integration time — know that you will need time to process all that you have received, and let it sink into your body and spirit and soul. You may not understand the energy that you have received, and that is fine; there is no need to intellectualize what happens when you receive from the trees, when you receive from Nature. The important thing is that you allow yourself to receive, and that you allow yourself to integrate that which you have received. This may take time; you may feel tired, hungry, needing to rest afterward, or you may not notice anything. Just be aware that time is needed, so you may find that your experiences with the trees, your experiences with Nature, go in spurts; you may find yourself very drawn to be out in Nature, and then you might find that you don't feel like going out for several days, or several weeks. This is natural, this is a natural cycle. You receive and then you integrate, you receive and then you integrate, you receive and then you integrate. This is all natural, this is all normal. Go with the flow, do what you feel you need to do.

This is all.

FOR MUCH OF the time that I had been out collecting tree stories this year, I had been approaching it as a kind of transaction: I had been told a tree had a story for me, then I went to receive it. It was very...professional. This experience with The Somerset Four was one of the first times that I started to feel more emotional toward the trees and connect with them in the same way that I might connect with another human being. My interaction with the trees was beginning to feel more personal, and less distant and professional.

I wondered if this was because I was unconsciously beginning to relax more as I connected with the trees: by this time, I had channeled 23 tree stories, and this was the 24th. I had more experience. The book was coming together. It was no longer this nebulous project that I wasn't sure whether or not I'd be able to complete.

In any case, this afternoon truly was a tipping point for me in my interaction with the trees: it was a move from professional interaction to personal engagement. I felt it within me as I revisited trees that I had received stories from earlier in the year. And I was beginning to feel that perhaps I hadn't shown enough gratitude for them: I had thanked them for their stories, yes, but perhaps I needed to leave them some kind of offering. I thought about making a pilgrimage to revisit each and every one of the trees in this book and offer more formal thanks, and maybe also a small crystal or something as a token of my gratitude. It now felt as though the words "thank you" weren't quite enough. They had given me so much: not just their stories, but some truly useful advice...and, of course, the basis for this book. They were helping not just me, but humanity.

I had noticed my need for integration time in my own mindset work that I did with myself: I would often go through periods of time where I would do daily mindset work with myself, shifting a number of beliefs every single day. And then I would go weeks, perhaps even a month or more, without doing any work with myself. It wasn't long before I realized that this was a pattern: a kind of ebb and flow of my inner work. I began to understand that the times when I wasn't doing any mindset work with myself were the times that my system was integrating the changes that I had made. It was my resting time, and then once everything had been integrated I naturally felt ready to do more.

WHAT ABOUT YOU? Do you experience ebbs and flows of

doing inner work, or in other areas of your life? Are you aware of the cycles you experience in your inner self?

Are there times when you feel really drawn to spend more time in Nature, and times when you don't? What are the times of the year that you prefer to be outdoors? I find that I spend more time outdoors in spring and autumn, and less in summer and winter when the weather is more extreme.

25

RAILWAY OAK

The day I went out to collect the next three stories was one of those days where I could hear the tree's story even before I reached it, as I had experienced in Savernake Forest in the days before Samhain. This was interesting to me because I had originally attributed this ease of channeling to the energy of Samhain, but perhaps it was simply because I was getting better at receiving the stories of trees: I had more experience now. I knew exactly where I was going, since I was very familiar with this trail, and as I approached the tree, I could sense his energy off in the distance. A story popped into my head, and I knew that it was *his* story and not my own thoughts.

I had finished collecting the stories of the Wiltshire trees and I was now back in the Surrey Hills. It was the last day of November, and the air was crisp and cool, with a clear sky. It felt very wintry, and it occurred to me that I had never walked on this trail at this time of year: I was usually there in the spring or the summer. I had parked my car in the nearby village, and then followed a narrow public footpath that ran between a house and some woodland before it crossed a little stream and then opened up into a field. I turned left and walked down the side of the field before turning right and heading up a gentle slope where a line of oaks separated the two fields. On my way, I passed another oak that I knew had a story for me. I paused, waiting to see if his story came first, but it did not, and I would later understand why.

I continued onward, up the side of the field, and when the path came to an end, I crossed a farm track and then continued on through another field, still heading slightly uphill. As usual, it was muddy. This farmland always seemed to be muddy, even in the drier months. The footpath ran down the left side of the field, which was bordered on the left by a small woodland. I could see the railway up ahead, running perpendicular to the footpath I was on. I continued up the footpath, climbed the stairs to cross the train tracks, and then went down the stairs on the other side.

The oak was right in front of me, to the left of the stairs, standing right next to the raised berm of the railway. I had passed this tree many times before on my walks, but I had never spoken with it. Now was the time to properly connect with the oak and get to know him. I felt a bit awkward reaching out to him because I had paid him so little attention on my walks. It almost felt like I had ignored him for years and I was now expecting something from him, though it was the old oak himself who had originally reached out to me to say that he had a story for this book.

It was summertime when you first realized that I was in your book. You were out on a walk, on a warm sunny day, clear skies

— much like this day, but warm instead of cold. And I said to you: "I am in your book." And you said you would come back. Many months have gone by since that day, and I know you have kept me in the back of your mind, and perhaps even chided yourself for not returning sooner.

I know it is important for me to say, to tell you now, that everything has its time, and everything has its place, and it is important that you are here now *in the chill of winter to receive my story. As you look up into my branches you can see that there are very few leaves still left on them. I do have more leaves than my neighbor oak, but there are not many left: they are scattered on the ground, all around me and I am going into that dormant time, that time of slowing down during the cold months. And the reason that it is important that you are here during this time is because I know other trees have spoken to you about the seasons, and the cycles, and the turning of the year, and I fear that this is something that you humans must hear time and time again in order for it to sink in.*

So, do not be bothered that my story may be similar to other stories that you have read, or received, or heard; because you may often sense a need to go within, to slow down, to quiet during these cold winter months. You may sense that you do not feel like going outdoors and walking and being active. You feel the need to be alone and silent, perhaps meditate, or read, or journal, or do the inner work. And this is fine, this is okay, this is appropriate.

We trees know that you people feel the need to go, go, go, and that is sometimes appropriate, and sometimes not. Every time there is a period of go, go, go there must be a time of rest, rest, rest. A time of action, a time of integration. A time of movement, a time of peace. And winter may be that time for some of you; it may not be for others. You may find that you require several periods of slowing down during the year, and this is fine.

We sense that this is a struggle for you people, and you feel that you must always be productive, that you must always be taking action, that you must always be doing something, you must always be working towards your goals, your things that you want to do, things that you want to achieve. Sometimes what is needed is to just be, *to just be who you are, where you are, what you are, how you are, right now in this moment, on this day. To relax, to rest, to integrate, but to be* aware *of who you are and what you are, and what you have, right now in this moment, instead of always looking to the future — to what you want to have, to what you want to be, to what you want to do.*

Be present in today.

We know that many people talk about being present in the moment and that can be very challenging for people. So, what I would suggest is to be present in today: what do you have today? What are you doing today? What are you being today? Who are you today? Forget the past, forget the future, just look at today. This period of time between the time you woke up this morning, and the time you will be going to bed this evening. Look at that, feel that, be that. It is just today.

Be grateful for what you have today. Be thankful for who you are today. Give gratitude for what you are doing today, for what you are capable of doing, for what you are able to do. Be thankful for having the time and the space in your life to do the things that you are doing today. Whatever that is, even if it is something that you do not enjoy doing, even if it is something that you need to do later and you wish you could procrastinate, or you want to procrastinate. Be grateful and focus on today.

All you have is today. We know this may sound overused perhaps, the concept that all you have is the present moment: the past no longer exists, the future does not yet exist, and yet they do, because if you step into your multi-dimensional self, everything exists all at once. That can be overwhelming, so we ask you to focus on today, how do you feel today? Not how do you want to feel — but how do you feel? Not what do you want to do today — but what are you doing today? Not who do you want to be — but who are you today? Who are you being today? Let go of wants, let go of wishes, let go of goals, let go of dreams, let go of visions. And practice this every once in a while. I do not say: practice it every day — you can if you want, of course, but just try it for once. Practice just being in today, being present in today.

This is something that you may wish to journal about: some of you may feel it easier to put your thoughts on paper, rather than to simply think them, or live them, or experience them. You might want to journal at various points throughout the day, or in the morning, or at the end of the day, to reflect on your experience of just being in today. Do whatever works for you, but we encourage you to try this just once, just once, and then pay attention to how it affects your life. What has changed as a result of this experience, and then decide whether you want to experience it again — this exercise of just being in today.

There is so much, so much focus on the past, so much focus on the future, I strongly encourage you to be in today, to live today, fully, in today. I wish you luck.

That is all.

EVERYTHING HAS ITS TIME; everything has its place. There is a time and a place for everything. Does this sound familiar? The Railway Oak's story was so similar in some ways to that of the Twin Sycamores in Avebury, and yet it took the concept a bit further, by urging us to be present in *today*. There were certain themes that the trees kept repeating: it was clear that they knew I sometimes needed to hear things over and over before they really sunk in.

I often spend little time outdoors in the cold, wet winter months. The past two years that I did the Walk 1,000 Miles

Challenge I started to get anxious in January and February because I wasn't getting any miles in. Because I have all the data from my walks in a spreadsheet to track my thousand miles, I can now see that while my walking starts out slow early in the year, it picks up during springtime and the warmer months, slowing down again as the end of the year approaches. It all evens out in the end, and I had achieved my goals in both years. My walking mimicked the seasons: the colder months are my times to go within, to stay indoors. And the warmer months are my times to go out, to explore.

That's why I find it so useful to keep track of things like my walking miles: I can see the patterns and I can stay on track by picking up the pace later in the year if I need to. Yet I always have the feeling of go, go, go when I'm tracking my progress toward a goal. The Railway Oak was quite right in saying that sometimes, we need to be focused simply on *today*.

There was recently a period of about a week or two when I was feeling really frustrated with certain things in my life. I had a meltdown — or two — and I was generally feeling lost and out of touch with myself. I had lost touch with my sense of unwavering self-trust, and it was kind of a bad moment in life. I booked a call with Lisa Wechtenhiser to get some help from my guides because I was so out of balance that I didn't even trust myself and my ability to receive the right message for myself. As usual, they came through with a simple solution: gratitude.

I do gratitude work on and off, in phases, like everything else I seem to do. But it had been months and months since I had last written a list of all the things that I was grateful for, and it showed. After the call, I dedicated a chunk of time in my morning routine each day that week to do some gratitude work. For me, "gratitude work" simply means making a list of ten or so things that I'm grateful for, and why. It's very simple, yet it has the power to completely change my attitude and my perspective on whatever it is that I'm struggling with.

The work helped me to focus on the present, see the things I already had, and to be truly grateful for them, rather than always looking to the future, to things that I wanted to be, do, and have. The shift was massive, and it completely transformed my perspective on the things I had been experiencing. It lifted me up out of a negative space and it got me back on track.

Sometimes, when things get overwhelming, it's incredibly helpful to just focus on *today*. Just do the things that need to be done today, and then take each day as it comes. It's like breaking down big goals into smaller milestones: it simply makes life doable.

How about you? Do you find it easy to focus on *today*, or do you find it difficult? Do you ever journal on what happens to you each day? How do you think that might be beneficial to your life? Is this something that you might be willing to try?

Do you ever do gratitude work? I know a lot of people have resistance to doing it, and if it's not for you, then don't feel an obligation to do it. But if you can give it a try, once in a while, perhaps when you're feeling down, see if it makes a difference in your attitude toward life. You might find it helpful.

26

BEARE GREEN OAK

After receiving the message from the Railway Oak, I lingered a while longer, then turned around and headed back toward the village. It was chilly out, and I still had two more trees that I wanted to speak with that day — one nearby, and another that I would have to drive to. This final oak, the Beare Green Oak, was located fairly near to the start of the trail, and I had passed it many times before on my walks, both on my own and in groups. Earlier this day, I had paused while approaching it, unsure as to whether I needed to receive its story first, or the Railway Oak's. It had been very clear in its response: Railway Oak was first. At the time, I was curious as to why there was a certain order to things, but it soon became apparent why this was so. The trees knew what they were doing.

I reversed the steps I had taken to get to the Railway Oak: I climbed back up the stairs and crossed over the train tracks, then went down the stairs on the other side. I climbed over the stile and then went down the first field, then the second. The border of trees was now on my right, and I easily identified the oak in question as I approached him.

The weather was still cool, crisp, and dry, and there was just one dog walker out, heading down the far side of the field. As always, I was conscious of any other people that might be around me, because I wanted to be uninterrupted when I received the tree's story. It was hard to receive a story if I wasn't relaxed. I was very aware of how close I was to the village, but it seemed to be a quiet weekday afternoon. Despite its proximity to the nearby neighborhood, I rarely crossed paths with another person on this trail, even on the weekends. I walked a full circle around the tree, looking for the best place to sit, then I settled down at its base.

I WILL NOT TELL you what so many other trees have told you, which is slow down, you move too fast. *But what I will tell you is that things often take — they often require — time and space. This is a lesson that you have learned, that you may continue to learn, that not everything happens in the timeframe that you would desire it. Let's take this book: perhaps you would have wanted to receive all the stories of the trees in one month, or in one season. But it has taken almost the course of the entire year to receive these stories: there have been different trees, in different places, and it has been important to receive different stories at different times of the year, as you have just learned.*

This is just one more perfect example of how some things — all *things perhaps — require time and space. And you must give yourself time and space if you want to achieve the things you want to achieve; if you want to experience the things that you want to experience. Some things take time. Some things take a longer time than you would expect, some things take less time than you would expect. This is all normal, this is all okay.*

The important thing is to recognize — to recognize that things take time. When you slow down, and you give yourself the space to open up and receive, to open up and experience, to open up and feel, this will lead you to new experiences, to new things, to new ways of being. And this requires space. And what we mean by space is slowing down, sitting still, just being, quieting your mind, journaling, meditating, sitting in silence, being still. And opening up to receive; to receive guidance from your higher self, to receive messages, to receive downloads, and this will help you connect to yourself, this will help you trust yourself, this will help you cultivate that inner-compass that can be life-changing.

This takes time, this takes space. And this is why my message is to remind you to give yourself space — alone time, self-care time — in which you can be quiet and be still, and relax and receive and connect. Give yourself permission to give yourself space. Give yourself permission to give yourself time. Give yourself permission to be still.

You may feel that stillness time is lost time — wasted time — because you are not being productive. On the contrary, stillness time is every bit as productive *as doing time. Give yourself permission to slow down, and be still, and make space.*

You may feel restless, you may want to move, you may want to get going onto your next thing. So, allow yourself to ease into this practice of being still and giving yourself space, and see if you can change your perspective. See if you can change your perspective so that you see stillness time as productive time, or whatever word you need it to be — valuable time, worthy time, useful time. Use whatever word you need to fully appreciate the value of this time and space that you give yourself.

It is important to give yourself time and space without sensory input, so you may think of doing a guided meditation, and while these are good, it is also good to be still without this type of auditory input. You may find it useful to do sensory deprivation activities such as a floatation tank, a place where you can go in silence, in peace, in darkness, and just rest and relax and just be. There are many ways that you can do this. You can simply meditate in the dark and silence at home. Whatever feels right for you. We encourage you to be still in all your senses, not just movement, but to be in silence and stillness and darkness — this will help you connect to yourself, your higher self, your inner compass, and it will open you up to new ways of being.

That is all.

I've always been the kind of person that needs a lot of alone time. I have an extensive morning routine where I do my inner work: I work on the lessons from my druid training course and I perform my sacred grove exercise. I journal, I do gratitude work, and I read whatever book I'm in the middle of. I do my mindset work to clear fears, blocks, and limiting beliefs. It looks a bit different every morning, but I have a set of activities that I choose from based on whatever it is that I feel I need on any given day. If I forego my morning routine for whatever reason, my day will feel a bit off and it will be harder for me to concentrate on my work. If I miss it for a number of days in a row, either because I'm traveling or not feeling well or because I'm busy with morning meetings, I feel very unsettled.

Giving myself the time and space to be alone and do my inner work helps me to feel grounded and connected with myself. It's helped me to get to know myself better and get aligned with creating the life I want to live. It's what helps me to be productive and get things done throughout the rest of the day — and yet I often feel guilty for setting aside so much time for myself.

However, I am still very much aware that my morning routine is what the oak called "doing" time. I'm very active during this part of the day: I'm not actually sitting still in meditation, silencing my mind and letting go of thoughts — I'm always *doing* something. Sitting in stillness is actually something that I find it a bit difficult to do, ven though it does form a brief part of my sacred grove exercise. I always feel like I need to take advantage of the time I have to do, do, do... something.

That's why it was so challenging for me when I channeled my Heart-centered Energy Work® process a couple of years ago: as I mentioned earlier, I literally had to sit in silence and wait to receive it, step by step, without knowing what was coming next. It was a true test of my self-trust. But I never would have received the process if I hadn't made the time and space to *be still*. In this case, being still was absolutely productive because it allowed the process to come through. In fact, I had been waiting for the process for a couple of months by that point, and the only thing that had been holding me back was the fact that I wasn't making time for stillness.

HOW ABOUT YOU? Do you find it easy to sit in stillness, or is it a challenge? If so, what are some ways you could add a bit of stillness to your life, even if it's just a few minutes? When would be a good time of day to do this? Remember, it doesn't have to be in the morning. In fact, some people have a shorter routine that they observe in both the morning and evening.

Do you make self-care a priority? What kinds of things

help you to feel like you're caring for yourself? Reading a book? Taking a bath? Sitting in the garden? Do you get enough self-care time in your life? If not, when could you add a bit of self-care to your life, even if it's just a few minutes?

27

WOLVENS LANE BEECH

This beech tree is located right off a byway in the Wotton Estate in the Surrey Hills, on one of my favorite walking routes. The beech first reached out to me early in the year, not long after I was first given the idea for this project. I was planning a circular walk near Dorking that passed by a sacred well and a lush waterfall, and this tree reached out to me with the usual words: "I'm in your book." I kept it in the back of my mind, passing it many times on my walks throughout the year, and I finally returned to collect its story at the end of November, just after receiving the stories of the previous two trees.

Despite this beech being present in the back of my mind all year, I'm sorry to say that this tree's story almost got lost in my files — not once, but twice. I was going through photos from the trees that I had taken throughout the year, and I came across one that I didn't recognize. I could see that the date was the same as the Railway Oak and the Beare Green Oak, which meant that it was taken when I was out collecting the last two stories for this book. At once, it came to me: it was the Wolvens Lane Beech. I went through my files, found my recording of its message, and sent it off to be transcribed. The second time this chapter got lost was when I compiled the document for export, and somehow the chapter didn't make it into the file. After going through my final review of this book, I realized something was missing: once again, it was the Wolvens Lane Beech.

This tree is located right off to the side of Wolvens Lane, which is a byway open to all traffic that stretches from the village of Wotton in the north to Coldharbour in the south. This beech sits on a fairly quiet part of the trail, at a crossroads where a footpath heads down towards Simon's Copse and Broadmoor. On the day I went to receive the beech's story, I parked near Broadmoor and walked up the hill toward the beech. Because I had never walked the trail in this direction, I wasn't fully sure I was in the right place. It all looked very different from this angle.

When I reached Wolvens Lane, I could see I had arrived at the exact point I had intended, and I walked around the beech, greeting it, before I settled in at its base. I felt very exposed, since I was sitting right on the side of a very wide trail, at a crossroads where people could approach from four different directions. It was certainly not the most private of places to receive a tree's story, but it was a weekday afternoon, and I hoped it would be quiet. Just seconds later, I heard voices as three people came walking up the same trail that I had. I pulled out my bottle of water and had a drink as I waited for them to pass. They crossed the byway and headed straight on down the trail. When I was positive they were out of earshot, I pulled out my phone and began to record the beech's story:

~

I WOULD SAY *I am surprised to see you. And yet, I knew I would see you again, and that you would come back to collect my story. You have walked by me many times since the first time I told you that I would be in your book, and that I had a story for you. And it is not by accident that you have returned to me near the end of the year, after receiving so many other tree stories.*

Many of the trees have been talking to you about slowing down, sitting, being still. This is all sound advice. And yet, I am here to talk to you about the journey. For this book has been a journey. It has been a journey for you as the collector of stories, and it is has been a journey for you as the reader of the stories. And it has been a journey for me and for all the trees. So I am here to remind you, at risk of sounding hmm... cliché, that life is a journey, that everything is a journey.

I know that the previous trees have spoken to you of things taking time and this is true, and we know that this can be frustrating to you. I encourage you to see life as a journey and everything as a journey: a journey of personal development, a journey of achieving your goals, a journey of working towards your dreams. So often you people focus on the end result, so often you focus on what you will get at the end *of the journey. I am here to remind you to focus on the path, to focus on the trail, to focus on all the little bits in between.*

It should be easy for you to understand this because when you go on your walks, the focus of the walk is not getting to the end: it is enjoying the path, it is enjoying the journey, it is enjoying the experience of the walk. So, why then can you not apply this to your life? To the rest of your life? To all the other things that you do?

I am going to say the words that you have heard so many times this year: slow down. Slow down and experience the path; slow down and experience the journey; slow down and experience the freedom of each step as it takes you forward. Or backwards. Or sideways. Or wherever you are going. Truly experience the path, truly experience each day, truly experience the process of getting from where you are to where you want to be. And be open to the fact that the destination may change. It may change once, it may change twice, it may change many, many times, along your path, along your journey. And this is fine. This is good, this is desirable.

It is desirable that you should be flexible, to flow with the changes of life. And yet that is not possible if you are only fixated on the end. And so I encourage you to focus instead on each single step. Each step on the way, each step on the path, each step on the journey. Take your steps one by one.

Focus on each step. Experience each step. Relish each step. Live each step.

Rather than seeing these steps as the necessary bother of getting from here to there, relish them as the main dish, the main course, the main part of your experience.

You have seen, when you go on your longer walking journeys, that when you get to the end, it is not what you expected: it is not what you hoped for, there are no fireworks and parties and celebrations. Yes, of course you can have your own personal celebration and perhaps you should, if you want to.

But on your longer walks you have seen that each step of the way, each day of the trail, is the core part of the experience, it is the main course, and you can apply that concept to the rest of your life. Each step of the way being the main course of your life, and not the end, not the destination, because your life will be full of destinations. It is all a path of cycles and returns. So it is vital that you enjoy each step of the way. Relish it.

You may be wondering: that sounds so easy, how do I do that?

It can take time out of each day, in the morning, in the afternoon, in the evening. In the morning and evening would be good, or perhaps just once a day, to do a daily review. What did you experience that day? What path were you walking? What actions did you take? How did you feel? What did you do? How did the steps that you took today contribute to your path, to your journey, to your experience of life?

You can spend some time reflecting or you can write them down in your journal, but do this once a day, whenever you feel is best. You could do it in the morning, reflecting on the previous day. You can do it in the afternoon, reflecting on the previous 24 hours. You can do it in the evening, reflecting on all the events that have occurred in your waking hours.

But focus on those steps, write them down in your journal, reflect on them. Focus on the steps that you took on your life's path, today. What they gave you, what they did for you, and how you felt about them and how they contributed to your overall journey.

Try this, and see how things change for you. Pay attention to the changes. Pay attention to how you feel differently. Pay attention to how you experience life differently.

Thank you. That is all.

OH, these trees knew me so well! I have the tendency to be so impatient: I set very clear goals for myself, I plan the steps I need to take to achieve those goals, and then I get very impatient about getting to the end result. I want the outcome *now*, and I rarely take the time to enjoy the journey of getting from here to there. And yet, so many of life's lessons are learned throughout the journey, and not upon achieving the end goal.

The Wolvens Lane Beech gave me the perfect example: my long-distance walks. The pleasure of walking, say, one hundred miles along the South Downs Way from Winchester to Eastbourne is not in arriving at the little snack bar at the end of the trail. It's in the process of walking the entire trail: the people I meet, the things I see, the challenge of walking day after day for an entire week. Somehow, I manage to forget this in my day to day life.

And the pleasure of writing this book was not in finishing the final draft so I could send it to my editor and eventually wrap up the project. It was in going out on my walks, in having the trees reach out to me and let me know they were in the book, and in eventually collecting their messages and putting them together to share with others. The pleasure was in the process: in the adventure and the discovery.

I get so frustrated when things don't work out as I planned, or when things don't go my way. I blame myself: what did I do wrong? What could I have done differently? What else should I be doing? Rather than welcoming the lessons, I criticize myself for not getting things right on the first try. And then I pick myself up, make some adjustments, and carry on.

The past decade of my life, ever since I left my first business, has been about making adjustments. I've done a massive amount of healing and personal development work, including hours and hours of mindset work with myself. I've released fears and blocks, and I've transformed my beliefs. Step by step, it's helped me to peel off layers of myself that weren't really me. Little by little, I've been working on removing the masks and getting back to the core of myself — my true self.

It's been a journey, and because I don't really know what's at the very core, I've been able to take it step by step. Sometimes, when we don't know what the end goal or the end result is, it makes it easier to enjoy the path to get there. Deep down, I know there's a part of me that knows what my true self is, but I'm not consciously aware of that: I'm still discovering it bit by bit. And with every layer that I peel off, it's exciting to see what's underneath. It's kind of like walking a path that spirals toward the center of myself. And of all the paths I've walked, this is the most satisfying of them all.

WHAT ABOUT YOU? Do you find it easy to focus on the journey, or are you so focused on the end result that you forget to enjoy the path to get there? What can you do to truly relish each step of your journey? What can you do to enjoy each step on your path to achieve your goals?

How do you feel about doing a daily review where you write about your day? How do you think that might change your life? When would be a good time to do this?

28

NEWLANDS CORNER YEW

I knew instinctively that the final tree in this book would be the very first tree, and that the stories of trees would come full circle when I revisited the very yew that had given me the idea for this book in the first place. It was December 21st — the winter solstice — and it had been almost a full year since I had first met the yew. I was fairly confident that he would be easy to find, but I ended up wandering around Newlands Corner for over an hour before I eventually discovered the exact grove where he was located. It had been winter when I first saw him, and it was winter once again, but somehow everything looked different.

It was a beautiful clear day, but it had been raining all week, and the trails were muddy. I tried to retrace the steps I had taken with the group when I went on the forest bathing Meetup, but I soon realized I had lost track of where I was in relation to the yew grove. We had made so many stops on the Meetup to focus on the smaller details of the forest, and I had failed to take in the bigger picture of the woods. Eventually, I crossed all the way over to a point that appeared to be where we had exited the woods to end up on the grassy hillside. From there, I turned around and tried to retrace my steps to the yew grove. And that's when I found him.

It was darker within the grove, despite it being a sunny afternoon. The woodland floor was carpeted with russet leaves from the deciduous trees in the forest. As soon as I entered the grove, I instantly recognized the ancient yew tree and I hurried across to greet him. It was like seeing an old friend. He had sent me on a mission to write this book, and I had learned so much. I was so grateful for having been given this idea and this opportunity, and I wanted him to get a sense of just how much it had changed me.

The yew stood straight and tall, with a second yew right next to him. Rather than standing next to him as I had first done when I met him, I circled around him and his companion yew before settling in to sit at the base of his trunk. I felt a great sense of friendship for this yew, despite only having seen him once before in my life. It was in part due to my sense of gratitude for being given this project, but it was also a result of how my relationship with trees, in general, had changed over the course of the year: I now saw them as specific individuals of a community, each with their own personality and spirit. I knew them as I knew the different people in my life.

I settled in at the base of his trunk, making myself comfortable. It was cold and damp on the forest floor, but I couldn't wait to reconnect with this yew. I was thrilled to hear his first words.

~

I KNEW *you would be back.*

The other trees weren't so sure, but I knew I had given the task to the right person. And I also know that this project — this book — is not what you expected. I know that it turned out to be very, very, different — different types of stories; different focus; different energy; different feel — to what you expected, to what you thought you would receive.

And this was an important part of your path, an important part of your journey, and an important part of the story, the overarching story for your readers, because sometimes things aren't what we expect, sometimes things don't work out the way we wanted them to, and sometimes we question: are we on the right path? Am I going in the right direction? Did I make the right decision? Am I where I am supposed to be right now, or should I be here, or should I be there, or should I be further... further ahead on my path?

And this is normal, and this is natural, and this is all a part of you trusting yourself, learning to trust yourself, and learning to be flexible and fluid and flow with the changes, to flow with the unexpected differences and to trust that all is well, while at the same time, working to achieve the things that you want to achieve, doing the things that you want to do, but having that flexibility, that flow, so that when things aren't what you expected you can flow around them, flow up over them, and envision yourself like the water, the water that rains down upon us, the water that flows through a stream. Moving water always finds its way, it always finds its path, it creates its own path.

There are many lessons to be learned from Nature. In this book you have learned from trees, and we have much wisdom, and if you were to write another book and another and another and continue to collect the stories of trees, you would have so many different messages and lessons and perspectives and things that you can do, and things that you can try, and it would be endless — it would be as many trees as there are on this planet, but that is not necessary. If you feel drawn to do so, you can do so, in the same way that you can, on your walks, reach out to trees, ask them if they have a message for you, and receive their message. And you can simply receive. It does not need to be made into anything; it does not need to be Volume II of this book. It does not need to be an encyclopedia of all the tree stories — it can simply be a message for you...or not.

You could take the list of activities and suggestions that the trees in this book have given you, and you could do them all and cross them off on your list, or you could do none of them, or you could do some of them. Or you could create your own things based on what you feel like doing, how you feel like connecting with the trees, how you feel like connecting with Nature, or even new ideas of things that new trees give you. You can do whatever you want, whatever feels right for you, there are no prescriptions, there are no laws, there are no shoulds, there are only coulds. You could do this, or you could do that. You might do this; you might do that.

There are only possibilities: possibilities for you on your journey to connecting with the trees, to connecting with Nature in all of its forms, in all of its realms, connecting with the plant realm and the animal realm and the mineral realm. You may feel more drawn to one than to the other. I suspect if you are reading this book it is because you feel drawn to the plant realm: to the green things, to the green spirits, and this is fine, and this is good, and we encourage this. And we also encourage connection with the animal realm and the mineral realm, because it is all valid and it is all good and it is all part of Nature, and it is all part of the ways that you can connect with yourself, through connecting with Nature. And the more that you slow down, and the more that you slow your speed, and the more that you learn to be still, in your life and in Nature, the easier it will be for you to connect with yourself and the easier it will be for you to build that inner trust, that inner sense of self-love and acceptance that some of the trees have spoken to you about.

I am so pleased that you have gone on this journey that I

sent you on, and I am so pleased that you are sharing this message with others, and I would encourage you — readers of this book — to please, please, please share this message with other people, in whatever way comes naturally to you. You can write about this in your journal, and get your clarity, and then talk about it with friends. You can blog about it, and you can do whatever feels right for you. But please, I encourage you: if you have felt touched by Nature, if there is something that you read in this book, or through something else, please share this message with others. Because the more people that get out in Nature, and the more people that connect with Nature and really build a relationship with Nature, the more we will experience harmony on this planet because, as you can see from this book, this has very much been about building a relationship with Nature in the same way that you would build a relationship with another human, or another animal.

This is a journey of building relationships, and any stories that you can tell people about building relationships with Nature will help others to build a relationship with Nature; and the more humans that deepen their connection with Nature and their relationships with the elements of Nature, the healthier this planet will be, the happier this planet will be; and it will lift the energy of this Earth and all of the living beings that inhabit it. It will lift the energy up into a new state of health and wellbeing and enlightenment and lightness of being and light energy.

We are here, and we are waiting. We will always be waiting.

And so we send this out to you as an invitation: an invitation to connect with us, to build a relationship with us, and in doing so to raise the vibration of the energy of this planet, and as you help yourself you will be helping every living thing on this Earth. That may seem impossible, it may seem strange, difficult, yet it is true. By helping yourself you will — little by little — raise the vibration of everything here, and the more people that do this, the more people that step into this, the more people that walk this path, bit by bit, little by little, everything will shine, and you will turn up the volume — the brightness — of the light that shines across this planet and things will begin to heal. Wellness, balance, and equilibrium will be restored. This is possible, little by little, bit by bit, with everyone doing their bit, everyone doing their part.

I hope you have enjoyed this journey and I hope you continue to take steps on this path, connecting with Nature, building relationships with Nature. It has been a pleasure to have had my part in stimulating this adventure, sparking the first step on this journey. I am so grateful that you have joined me, and we the trees, we thank you, thank you, thank you, thank you.

That is all.

THIS WAS the perfect ending to my journey of collecting tree stories — except it wasn't the ending, it was simply the completion of a circle, the turning of the year, one turning of the spiral on my journey to building relationships with the trees and, in turn, to building my relationship with myself. I had never really seen my relationship with Nature as part of my personal development, and yet I was now aware that was very much the case. The more time I spent outdoors, the more I felt connected to my inner self.

I truly believe that the more we connect to our true, authentic selves, the happier we'll be. We'll be walking our true path in life, consciously creating the experiences that we want to have. Too many people are stuck in a rut, having made life decisions that weren't aligned with what they truly wanted to experience, and now they feel stuck, frustrated, and hopeless.

I've been there. About eleven years ago, I was deeply

unhappy with my life. I felt like there was no way out of the situation I'd gotten myself into. But that wasn't true: I simply didn't like the decisions I would need to make to get myself on another track. They were tough decisions: I needed to end a relationship that I had been in for ten years, and I needed to end my involvement with a company I had co-founded.

After completely upending my life, I found myself with a blank canvas, which was quite honestly terrifying. I spent over a year experimenting with new paths. There were so many things I *could* do, but which one of them was the *right* thing for me? In the end, I understood that I needed to just pick one thing and try it, then go from there. Since then I've learned the importance of taking just one step, even if I don't know where it will lead me. I don't need to know where the end of the path lies for me to start walking. The good thing about walking is that you can take a step in a new direction at any moment — you just need to make the conscious decision to do so.

And so, I invite you to take the next step on the journey to the center of yourself: try some of the things that the trees have suggested in this book. Adapt them to make them more personalized for your interests and needs. Develop your relationship with Nature so that you can develop your relationship with yourself. As the Newlands Corner Yew confirmed, this won't just help you personally — it will help raise the vibration of the entire planet. Because the more people who do this work with themselves, the more evolved we'll become.

PART III

EPILOGUE

If there is one overarching theme for the messages I received from the trees, it is this: *slow down, you move too fast.* I learned that life is more about *being* rather than *doing.* We tend to place value only on the things we *do*: the actions we take, the goals we achieve, the results we get. Over the course of this year, I learned to value how I *be* (yes, I'm aware that sounds grammatically weird): the feelings I experience, the energy that flows through me, the thoughts that course through my mind.

As I mentioned earlier in this book, I've had an extensive morning routine for a couple of years now, where I spend the first 2-3 hours of each day in meditation or spiritual practice, doing gratitude work, journaling, or reading. In previous years, my time of inner focus or *being* time was compartmentalized within this morning routine...though as I wrote this book, I became aware that there's a lot of *doing* in my morning routine as well.

My journey of collecting the tree stories for this book has taught me to take my inner work and my *being* time outdoors and spend more time in stillness when I'm out walking, rather than pushing to get my miles in before sundown. I learned to keep track of the things I experienced when I was at rest in the woods by journaling about them, in addition to tracking my miles for my Walk 1,000 Miles challenge. I learned that sitting in Nature is just as valuable as walking through Nature. *Being* is just as important as *doing*.

And speaking of the Walk 1,000 Miles challenge: I decided that I won't be participating in it again in 2019. For the past two years, it helped me to get outdoors and spend more time in Nature, but it also encouraged me to move, move, move through Nature. For 2019, I decided to motivate myself to spend more time being still outdoors, and my challenge for myself will be based on the number of days I spend in Nature, rather than the number of miles I walk. This way, I'll be able to push myself to spend more time outdoors, but the focus will be more on inner time, or *being* time, rather than on getting the miles in.

I want to focus on deepening my relationship to Nature: not just with the trees, but with other plants, and animals, and minerals. I want to connect more with different types of Nature spirits. I want to *be* with Nature.

As part of my Bardic Grade review for OBOD, the druid order I belong to, I had to write about my gift to the world, and what it is. It took me most of the year to understand what my gift to the world is: it's my writing, specifically my books about Nature. In January 2018, just one month after beginning the Bardic Grade OBOD course, I received the idea for this book. My journey of collecting the trees' stories paralleled my work through the Bardic Grade, and I received the final chapter from the Newlands Corner Yew just about the same time that I was finishing up my Bardic Grade coursework.

This book has been much like my walking books in that

it is a very experiential book, with the main difference that it forced me to slow down and spend more time being still in Nature, whereas in previous years my focus was on my walking: on moving through Nature; the more miles, the better. This shift from doing to being was very much aligned with my work in the Bardic Grade, which encouraged me to slow down and reconnect with myself and get to know new layers of myself, as I related to Nature.

I'm very excited to share this gift with the world, to help encourage others to slow down and experience Nature in new ways. I see my role here not just as an author — as the person who wrote this book and put it out there to be read — but as a facilitator of *experience*: the experience of deepening your relationship with yourself through deepening your relationship with Nature. I hope that it opens you up to new ways of connecting with Nature and of connecting with yourself.

1

CONNECT

In the interest of making it as easy as possible for you to try out and play with different ways of connecting with Nature and the trees, I've compiled a list here of everything the trees suggested. I'm also including some journal prompts of my own to help you dig a bit deeper and to process your experiences. All of this is, of course, totally optional. This is not a list that you're meant to work through, one by one, in the exact order...unless that's your preferred way of doing it. There's no right or wrong way to do this: you can dip in and out as you like. Do the activities that you most feel drawn to.

If you'd like to take this work further, I've expanded this section into a full workbook, where you can not only work through the activities suggested by the trees, but you'll also have space to journal and write about your experiences. You can purchase that workbook wherever you bought this one, or visit my website to learn more.

I've also created a little online space with guided meditations and other materials that will help you to work through some of these activities. You can access these free resources by going to http://hollyworton.com/trees.

Finally, if you do decide to write about your relationship with Nature or your experiences with any of these activities, please reach out to me and let me know. I'd love to hear from you. You can use the contact form on my website: http://hollyworton.com/contact.

I'd also love for you to share your experience with Nature online, whether that's on your blog, in a video, on social media, or wherever. I invite you to use the hashtags #iftreescouldtalk and #italktotrees. When people share their experiences in Nature, it will inspire others to do the same.

Lone Oak

> Go to the woods, or to a place in Nature. Stop, sit, be still, and *experience* the place: open your ears, open your eyes, touch the things around you, smell them. Take in all the sounds that you hear: both human-made and Nature-made.
>
> You might want to take a journal with you to write down everything that you see, hear, smell, and feel.
>
> Touch the trees when you're out walking; make physical contact as you greet them.
>
> Pay attention to the differences between the trees in the forest: the different yews, the different oaks, the different hollies (or whatever types of trees you have in your

area). How does the energy of each one feel? How is each one different from the others? Were you able to get a sense of their different personalities? Their individuality?

Journal Prompts – Before the Experience

- Do you spend much time outdoors in Nature?
- Do you go on walks in Nature, or do you spend quiet time sitting outside?
- Do you usually find yourself moving through Nature, or being still in Nature?
- Do you ever stop and take the time to really observe all the sounds of the outdoors?
- If you were to plan an excursion somewhere where you could sit in stillness in Nature, where would you go? To a park or to a woodland? Or somewhere else, like a river, a lake, or an ocean?
- Do you prefer cozy, closed-in views like the ones you get in a forest, or do you prefer expansive views like you can find on the coast?
- Can you identify the different species of trees in your area? Would you like to be able to do this, maybe by purchasing a guidebook to trees in your area?
- Do you ever stop to notice the differences between the individual trees of each species and compare two oaks or two yews, for example?

Journal Prompts – After the Experience

- What human-made sounds did you hear?
- What Nature-made sounds did you hear?
- Did you notice more sounds when you were

sitting still in the woods compared to when you were walking?
- How did you feel when you were listening for the sounds?
- Did you hear anything that you couldn't recognize?
- How did you feel when you touched the trees as you greeted them?
- Did it make you feel more connected to the plant life around you?
- What did you notice when comparing different trees of the same species?
- How did they differ? How were they similar?
- Did you have a favorite species or individual tree? Why?
- How did you feel when you were doing this activity?
- Is this something that you'd like to do again?

Chalice Well Yews

Seek out places that have a "special" sort of energy or go to a place in Nature where you feel drawn to. Sit still, and bathe in the energy of the place. Meditate if you like. Focus on how you *feel* in this place, so you can recognize this feeling in other places. You might find it useful to bring a journal and write down everything that you feel in this space. Remember to give thanks to the place before you leave.

Make physical contact with the trees: touch their bark,

brush your hand across their leaves. Get to know each tree as an individual: start with one type of tree, such as a yew. Touch its bark, smell its bark, smell the leaves and the ground at its base. Use all your senses to connect with the tree. Hug the tree, sit with your back against it, walk around it in a circle and look at it from all angles.

Repeat with other trees of its type and really sense the difference between each individual within the same species. Repeat the process with other species of trees: oaks, hollies, whatever type of tree you want.

Journal Prompts – Before the Experience

- Have you ever visited a place where you felt a very special kind of energy?
- Do you know of any places out in Nature that have a sacred feel to them?
- Have you ever visited them with the intent to just bathe in the energy, or do you feel like you have to do something special while you're there?
- Is this something you'd like to try? If so, where would you go? List all the places you can think of where you feel a "special" kind of energy.
- How do you know that these places are different?
- How do you feel when you're there? How would you describe the energy?

Journal Prompts – After the Experience

- What was it like to use all your senses to connect with the trees?
- How did you feel during this activity?

- Do you feel a greater sense of closeness to the trees now that you've connected with them in this way?
- What have you learned from the experience?
- Have you ever felt like you weren't alone when you were out in Nature, and yet couldn't see anyone else around?
- How does this make you feel? Are you curious, or frightened?
- If you feel uncomfortable when this occurs, what might make you feel more at ease?
- How often do you actually make physical contact with the trees you pass on your walks, whether it's in a park, in a garden, or in a forest?
- Do you ever touch them? Do you reach out to feel their bark, their leaves, or their fruits?
- How do you feel about making more physical contact with the trees you see?
- Are you able to easily see the different trees as individuals?
- Can you really differentiate between the trees in a woodland, or do they all look the same to you?

Juniper Bottom Yews

Step off the trail you're walking on, or the route you have planned. (Note that in the UK, it's best to try this on open access land, where there are many little trails all around and it's legal for you to step away from the public rights of way.) Discover new things: explore where another path goes. Really see all the options you have available to you.

Follow your intuition. Look beyond the path and pay attention to what's on either side of the trail. Practice being alert, aware.

Cultivate a sense of adventure when you're out in Nature: try new things and new trails.

Journal Prompts – Before the Experience

- Do you consider yourself to be a flexible person?
- Do you find it easy to change plans? Can you easily deviate from your planned path?
- How does it feel when you change your itinerary or stray from your intended path? Does it make you feel out of control, disorganized, or something else?
- If this is something that you find difficult, would you like to be more flexible?
- What about options? Do you usually take the time to see all the options you have available to you, or do you impulsively choose the first that you see?
- How would you feel about taking more time to make your decisions?
- How do you make your decisions: with your head or with your intuition?

Journal Prompts – After the Experience

- How did you feel about veering off from the path you had planned, or the trail you were walking?
- What was it like to explore new trails that you weren't familiar with?

- Was it easy to follow your intuition and try new paths?
- What did you discover when you looked at the things on both sides of the trail?
- What was different about this experience?
- What was it like to be more adventurous in the outdoors?
- What did you do differently?
- What else would you like to experiment with?
- How could you add even more adventure to your time in Nature?

~

Windmill Hill Sycamore

Open your mind to the possibility of magic: to the Nature spirits and to other dimensions. Pay attention to the times when you're out in Nature and you sense there is someone or something nearby, even if you do not see anything with your eyes.

Respect Nature in all its territories: the plant realm, the animal realm, and the mineral realm. Pay attention to your attitude as you walk in Nature.

Pay attention to where you tread: the soil, the mosses, the little plants on or alongside the trail. Be conscious of where you place your feet.

Journal Prompts – Before the Experience

- Do you believe in the multiverse? Why or why not?
- How do you feel about the possibility of the existence of Nature spirits, such as fairies and other elementals?
- Do you think it's possible that these beings exist, either within our own dimension or outside of it?
- Are you open to the idea of setting the intention to connect with these beings and see what happens? Or would you rather just leave them alone for now, and hope that they do the same?
- Are you open to the possibility of experiencing magic in your life?
- Do you ever sense that there are unseen beings around you when you're in the outdoors?
- How do you feel about that?
- Are you afraid of things that you cannot see, or are you excited about the possibility of getting to know them?
- What's your attitude as you walk in the outdoors?
- Do you ever ask permission to enter a place in Nature, or do you boldly step forward as though you were entitled to be there?

Journal Prompts – After the Experience

- How has your attitude changed when you walk in Nature since you began reading this book and doing these activities?
- How often do you pay attention to where you place your feet when you're walking in Nature?

- Do you try to avoid stepping on plants if possible?
- Have you ever found yourself apologizing to some living thing that you've stepped on?

Alton Priors Yew

Seek out ancient trees and visit them. If you know of a local forest that has particularly large or veteran trees, go to see them. If you do not know of such a place, do some research online and visit them. Tune into the energy of the place where they are located. Bring attention to the trees in whatever way you like: take photos and share them online, blog about your experience, create a video with the tree. Encourage others to visit ancient trees, too.

Cultivate a deep respect for Nature and focus on building a sense of harmony with the natural world. Remember to give thanks for the experiences you have.

Journal Prompts – Before the Experience

- Do you feel that a being (whether animal, plant, or mineral) is due more respect simply because it's older?
- Or do you believe that all beings deserve the same respect simply because they are alive and are a part of this world?
- Do you believe something else entirely?
- Do you hold the same hope as the Alton Priors

Yew does for the future of humanity's relationship with Nature?
- Do you think it's possible for humans to rebuild a new sense of harmony with Nature?
- Do you have hope for the future of our planet?
- How long do you think it might take us to regain a deep sense of respect for and connection with Nature? How many generations will it take?
- Finally, do you know of any ancient trees in your local area that you could visit? If not, have you done the research to find some? When would you like to go see them?

Journal Prompts – After the Experience

- Which ancient trees did you visit?
- What were they like?
- How did you feel when you were with them?
- Did you feel more respect for them because of their great age?
- Does spending time in Nature fill you with a sense of harmony?
- Do you feel a greater sense of respect and connection to the natural world since doing these activities?

Windmill Hill Hawthorn

Find your place in the world: travel, visit, experience, connect, dream, read.

Identify the places where your heart guides you to go: start connecting with them, visit them. When you go there: be still, be quiet, and experience the site with all of your senses. Sense, smell, hear, feel the place in every way. Become treelike in that place.

Journal Prompts – Before the Experience

- Have you found your place in the world, your heart place? If so, how did you find it?
- Do you have more than one?
- How does it make you feel?
- Are you living there, or is it a place you visit?
- If you have not yet found your heart place, your place in the world: which places are you drawn to?
- Which places would you like to explore? Where does your heart guide you to visit? Where do you dream of going?
- Which places have you always wanted to visit?
- What parts of the world do you find fascinating?

Journal Prompts – After the Experience

- What did you experience when you went to one of these places that you feel drawn to? What was it like? How did you feel? Will you be returning there soon?
- What do you think of this advice to become "treelike"?
- Do you find it easy to slow down and sense the things around you? Or are you constantly moving, taking action, doing things?

Avebury Beeches

Find a wishing tree in your area, or if you cannot find one, visit a sacred spring or well and see if there is a wishing tree there. If not, ask one of the trees near the spring if you can use it as a wishing tree. Tie a ribbon on the wishing tree or cloutie tree, and consciously harness the power of the tree when you make your wish. Ask the tree for help in making your dream come true. Always remember to give thanks to the trees for their help.

Journal Prompts – Before the Experience

- Have you ever seen a wishing tree? If so, have you ever made a wish while tying a ribbon on a branch?
- What types of things have you wished for?
- What types of things *could* you wish for?
- Did you ever realize that you might elicit the spirit of the tree to help you to make your wish come true?
- Do you think that asking the tree for assistance might help you to make your intentions stronger?

Journal Prompts – After the Experience

- How did it feel to consciously ask the tree for help when you made your wish?
- Could you sense the power of the tree's energy?

- Would you like to do this again, either with the same tree or with a different tree?
- What other things could you ask the trees for help with?

Fulbrook Oak

Pay attention to the trees that you pass when you go about your day: whenever you're out walking, or cycling, or driving.

Sit with your back against a tree trunk. Relax, connect, feel their energy through your back and up or down your spine. Allow their energy to flow into your body, and feel their strength. Connect with the life force energy and feel it in your body. Feel it in your heart. Receive. Always remember to give thanks to the trees for their help.

Journal Prompts – Before the Experience

- Do you really notice the trees around you when you're out walking, cycling, or driving?
- Do you ever sit or stand with your back against a tree trunk?
- What do you feel when you connect physically with a tree in this way?
- Have you ever noticed any kind of energy flowing from the tree through the back of your heart center?

Journal Prompts – After the Experience

- What was it like to connect with the energy of the tree?
- How did it feel when you allowed it to flow through you?
- Could you feel it in your heart?
- Were you able to allow yourself to fully receive?
- Is this something that you'd like to repeat, either with the same tree or with other trees?

Peper Harow Yew

Whenever you see an ancient yew (or other veteran trees that may exist in your region), sit and soak up the energy of the place. Feel the sacred energy of that site. Remember to give thanks to the place for its energy.

Journal Prompts – Before the Experience

- Can you sense when you're at a sacred site?
- Why do you think these places were chosen for worship in ancient times?
- What is it about the energy there that you think draws people to these particular sites?
- Do you believe in ley lines, or do you think they're something that was made up to connect the dots of the numerous sacred sites that are scattered all over the world?

Journal Prompts – After the Experience

- When you went to visit the ancient tree, were you able to feel the sacred energy of the place?
- Did you feel yourself receiving the energy? What else did you feel?
- Did you sense anything else there? Did it feel like a sacred site?
- Is this something that you'd like to repeat, either in the same place or somewhere new?

Ranmore Maple

Settle down against a tree and close your eyes and open your ears. Take in all that you hear, and resist the temptation to open your eyes when you hear an unfamiliar sound (obviously, be safe while doing this). If you find this difficult, set a timer for one, three, five, or more minutes. Start with whatever feels like a stretch. Perhaps take a journal with you to write down your observations once you open your eyes and finish the exercise.

Journal Prompts – Before the Experience

- Do you feel safe when you're alone in Nature?
- Do you feel safe enough to sit in silence with your eyes closed?
- Do you think you would be able to keep your eyes closed, even if you heard a sound that you couldn't identify?
- How do you feel about the maple's suggestion of stretching your comfort zone so that you can

expand your sense of safety as you fully
experience the woods?

Journal Prompts – After the Experience

- How did you feel when you closed your eyes in the woods?
- Did any fears come up for you?
- Were you able to keep your eyes closed, even when hearing an unfamiliar sound?
- What was the longest time you were able to keep your eyes closed for?
- How long would you like to try for the next time?
- Most importantly, what did you hear when your eyes were closed that you hadn't noticed when they were open?
- Is this something you'd like to repeat, either in the same place or somewhere new?

Ranmore Oak

Take your troubles, sadness, difficulties, and stresses to a tree. Sit on the ground against a tree, or stand next to it and hug it, or stand up with your back against the trunk. Imagine your worries and stress flowing out of your body and into the tree. Sense the tree absorbing the energy and carrying it down into the roots and into the earth, where it is transformed into neutral energy. Do this on a regular basis, whenever you're feeling unhappy or unwell. Remember to give thanks to the tree for its help.

See http://hollyworton.com/trees for a guided meditation you can download, which will help you with this.

Journal Prompts – Before the Experience

- Have you ever had a difficult conversation with someone when you were out in Nature, perhaps while sitting underneath a tree?
- Were you aware that the trees might be able to help you through your troubled times?
- How do you feel about the idea of taking your worries to the trees?
- Do you have a particular tree in mind that you'd like to ask for help with this?

Journal Prompts – After the Experience

- When you took your troubles to a tree, which issues did you bring to it?
- How did you feel when you were doing this activity?
- Was it easy for you to visualize sending your troubles to the tree to be absorbed?
- How did you feel afterward?
- Is this something you would like to try again?

Grandfather Tree

Sit in silence or meditate: slow down and listen to your inner guidance. Feel your body slow down as you tune into your own inner signals. Go within. Trust yourself. Remember, this is the biggest gift you can give yourself.

Try the mind decluttering meditation to clear your mind of thoughts and open up to hear your inner voice.

Find your own Grandfather Tree and make contact with it. Trust that you have found the right tree.

Journal Prompts – Before the Experience

- Do you fully trust yourself? On a scale of 1 to 10, with 10 being highest, how much do you trust yourself?
- Do you trust the decisions you make, or do you constantly second guess yourself?
- Do you believe that it's safe for you to trust yourself?

Journal Prompts – After the Experience

- What was it like to slow down and open up to your inner wisdom?
- How did it feel?
- Did you receive any guidance or messages?
- Did you come to any new awareness?
- Were you able to trust these messages?
- Did you find your own Grandfather Tree?
- Was it a tree you were already aware of, or is it a new one you met while doing this activity?
- Did you trust that you found the right one, or did you question yourself?
- Did you try the mind decluttering meditation? How many times did you try it? Did it help you

to get things out of your head and into a system for getting them done?
- Do you feel different now that you've cleared your head? Is it easier to hear the voice of your intuition?
- Do you think you'll continue using the mind decluttering meditation to keep your head clear of unnecessary information?

The Grandmothers

Perform the tree visualization (see http://hollyworton.com/trees for a guided meditation you can download, which will help you with this).

Work on your sense of self-trust, self-love, self-acceptance, self-esteem, self-confidence, self-value, and self-worth. Do what you can to improve these areas of your life.

Choose power.

Declare:

"I choose power for the good. I choose to step into my personal power. I am ready, willing, and able to step into my personal power and to live a life where I am grounded in my personal power, which I choose to use for the good."

Journal Prompts – Before the Experience

- How do you feel about the concept of personal power? Do you think power is good or bad?
- Do you feel powerful or powerless in your life?
- Have you ever felt like you were a victim of your circumstances?
- Have you ever felt that bad things just happened to you, and that you were powerless to do anything about them?
- How do you think it might feel to flip all this on its head and step into your own power?
- How do you feel about taking the oath of The Grandmothers?

Journal Prompts – After the Experience

- How did you feel when you said the declaration?
- What was it like to choose power?
- How powerful did you feel before making the declaration, and how did you feel afterward? Was there a shift?
- What else can you do to fully step into your personal power?
- How else can you choose power in your life?
- What can you do to cultivate your sense of self-trust, self-love, self-acceptance, self-esteem, self-confidence, self-value, and self-worth?
- If you choose *not* to take the oath of The Grandmothers — why is this? Are you afraid of something? Why do you think it doesn't feel right to you? Do you think that you might do it in the future?
- What was the tree visualization like? How did it feel?

- What type of tree did you choose to be, and why?
- What was it like to feel the strength, the power, and the energy of yourself as a tree?

The Three Witches

Open your mind to what Divine feminine power might look like or feel like, and ask a tree to help you step into it. Remember to give thanks to the tree for its help.

Journal Prompts – Before the Experience

- How do you feel about this concept of Divine feminine power?
- Is it something that you resonate with?
- Is it something that you're willing to accept into your life?
- Are you willing to tap into this energy, and to help others in your life cultivate?
- If you don't like the terms "feminine" and "masculine" energy, what words do you prefer?
- What do you think Divine feminine power might look like? Feel like?
- Do you believe in the power that you have as an individual to help change the world?
- If not, what would you need to believe in order to truly feel the power you have inside you to change things, even on a small scale?

Journal Prompts – After the Experience

- How did you feel when you asked the tree to help you to step into your Divine feminine power?
- The Three Witches said that it was *delicious* energy: were you able to sense that? How else would you describe it?
- How has your life changed since you asked for this help?

Sacred Springs Sycamore

Go to places of special energy and open yourself up to the magic of the land: to the possibility of connecting with the elementals and the Nature spirits. Remember to give thanks to the place for the experience, and for whatever else you may receive.

Help them and help Nature by caring for the land: recycling, conserving energy, leaving a lighter footprint. Change your life and your habits to help care for the Earth.

Journal Prompts – Before the Experience

- What more can you do to care for the land and our Earth? You probably already recycle at home, so what else could you do?
- How else can you be more respectful to Nature?
- How can you change your life to show more respect for our Earth?
- What habits can you change?

- What things can you do differently?
- What actions can you take — big or small — to help the planet?
- Are there any sacred springs in your area? If you're not aware of any, look for them online and identify where some might be.
- Do you believe in elementals and Nature spirits?
- Are you open to the possibility of believing in them?
- Do you sense when certain places have a magical feel to them?
- Why do you think this is? What do you think is going on there?

Journal Prompts – After the Experience

- Where did you go that was a place of special energy? Did you find a sacred spring?
- Did you feel the presence of any Nature spirits while you were there?
- Did the place have a magical feel to it?
- What actions have you taken to better care for our Earth?
- What more could you do to help our planet?

White Road Oak

Slow down and experience the forest with all your senses: smell the leaves, the rotting logs, the moss, the tree trunks, the air, the earth. Play with your senses in the woods.

Bring the children (and other adults!) in your life to smell the forest, touch the forest, and connect with the forest using their senses. Learn how to forage, and teach them to do it, especially when the berries are ripe. Ask them how they feel as they connect with each tree: ask them if each tree feels different, and ask them how it feels. Make a game of it (even with the adults!).

Journal Prompts – Before the Experience

- What are your dominant senses?
- Do you ever take the time to focus on the smells of the forest?
- Do you ever pick up some damp fallen leaves or a tuft of moss to smell them? Have you ever bent down to smell a rotting stump?
- What can you do to encourage other people in your life — especially children — to connect more deeply with Nature?

Journal Prompts – After the Experience

- If you made an effort to slow down, what did you experience?
- What smells did you discover?
- What senses do you use less often when you're in the outdoors? How can you use them more often?
- If you did the exercise, and invited someone else out to experience Nature, what was it like to take children (or other adults) out into the woods?
- Did you make a game of connecting with the trees? What did they think?

- How did you feel when you were playing with them?
- What other things could you do to help the children (and other adults) in your life connect with Nature?
- What other people in your life could you invite to share this experience with you?

Savernake Beech

Visit the same site at different times of the year. What do you see, smell, feel, hear? Feel the energy of the place with your body, and also touch the textures of the tree bark, the leaves, and the earth. Are there any fruits, flowers, fungi? What animals are around?

See if you can connect with one particular tree throughout the four seasons; see how that tree looks and smells and feels. See if that tree's energy shifts throughout the year.

Observe other people at this site and see how they experience the location throughout the different seasons: do they walk faster in the winter, and do they linger less?

Get a journal or notebook and dedicate several pages to each place, writing down as much as you can each time you go. Visit this site at least four times a year, one for each of the seasons, or turn it into a special pilgrimage that aligns with the wheel of the year: the solstices and equinoxes, and the midseason holidays on February 1,

May 1, August 1, and October 31. Put this in your calendar to make sure you remember to do it, since this is an ongoing activity.

Journal Prompts – Before the Experience

- Are there certain places in Nature that you naturally tend to visit many times throughout the year?
- Have you ever stopped to record your experiences, or to compare what it's like in the different seasons?
- How do you think it might deepen your connection to those places if you were to journal about what each experience is like?
- If you were to pick just one place to record your experiences and observations throughout the seasons, where would you go?

Journal Prompts – After the Experience

- What was it like to visit the same site throughout the year?
- Where did you go?
- What did you experience?
- What did you learn?
- How did you experience Nature in the different seasons: how did you feel?
- Do you prefer one season to the other? Which is your favorite season?
- What is your order of preference for all four seasons?
- Did you visit your site on the pagan festivals, or at random times throughout the year?

- If you went there on the pagan festivals, did you sense anything different on those dates?
- Is this something that you would like to repeat next year, whether in the same place or in a different location?

Pointing Oak

Put a small rubbish bag in your backpack so you can easily pick up garbage and plastic that you find in the woods. Do it: pick up the plastic and the rubbish that you find out in Nature. Treat this like it's not optional: that it's simply impossible to *not* pick up rubbish.

When you bring plastic bottles or other packaging into the woods, always be sure to put them safely inside your pack, and not in an outside pocket where it might fall off.

Never, ever intentionally leave your garbage and other plastics in Nature.

Journal Prompts – Before the Experience

- Do you carry a rubbish bag around with you when you go out into Nature?
- Do you ever pick up trash that other people have left behind?
- Are you willing to help to clean up the woods? If so, what are you willing to do? How often are you willing to do it? Are you willing to treat it like it's not an option to *not* pick things up?

Journal Prompts – After the Experience

- How do you feel when you pick up rubbish in Nature? Are you happy to do it, or is it an annoyance to you?
- Have you made it a habit to clean up the woods and other natural spaces?
- What else could you do to help rid the woodlands of plastic and rubbish?

Savernake Queen Oak

Find your joy in Nature: walking, running, cycling, meditating, or something else. Do it: make it happen on a regular basis, and really feel the joy in your body. Give yourself permission to have these experiences and make this a priority in your life.

If you haven't yet found your joy in Nature, try just one thing. Experiment. Keep trying things until you find it.

Journal Prompts – Before the Experience

- Have you found your joy in Nature? What is your joy in the outdoors? How do you feel joy in the outdoors?
- If you haven't found your joy in Nature, what types of outdoor activities are you drawn to doing?
- What new things do you feel like trying?
- How would you like to play in the outdoors?

Journal Prompts – After the Experience

- What is your joy in Nature? Is it walking, meditating, cycling...or something else?
- How do you feel joy in the outdoors?
- Is your joy in doing these activities alone, or with others?
- If you have found your joy, do you actually make it a priority in your life?
- How often have you made it a priority to experience your joyful activities in Nature?
- How do you feel about doing it: do you feel guilty, or are you able to enjoy these activities free from guilt?
- Do you do it on a regular basis? If not, what can you do to make it happen more often?

Western Hemlock

Appreciate the beauty of all trees. Be thankful for them all, both native and non-native trees. See them as individuals.

Pay attention to your attitude as you walk through commercial forests and native forests. See the beauty in the forest, in their service, in their uniformity. Pay attention to the life in the forest: what birds can you hear?

Do what you need to do to change your perspective on

commercial forests: feel respect for these trees; show your respect for them.

Remember to thank the trees that have given their lives for the products that we use: furniture, paper, cardboard, etc. They are providing a service to us; thank them for their service.

Journal Prompts – Before the Experience

- How did you feel about non-native forests before reading this chapter?
- Were you aware of having less respect for non-native trees, or was this not an issue for you?

Journal Prompts – After the Experience

- What was it like to visit the commercial forest?
- Were you able to put any negative attitudes aside and appreciate their beauty?
- What is your current attitude toward commercial forests and non-native trees?
- How do you feel about giving thanks for the products that we use that come from trees? Have you started doing this?
- Has it made you more aware of the origin of these products?
- Has it made you more aware of your consumption of these products?
- Have you changed your habits around using paper and cardboard products?

King of Limbs

Find the places in Nature that feel like a special bubble. Open up to receive the energy of the place. Keep your mind distracted by looking at a map or your phone or by writing in your journal. Stay as long as you like and know that when you begin to feel restless it is time to move on. Remember to give thanks to the place for the experience, and for whatever else you may receive.

Journal Prompts – Before the Experience

- Have you ever felt a strange energy like I did when I was at King of Limbs? How have you responded?
- If you've never experienced something like this, what do you think you would have done if you had felt the strange energy I experienced near the old oak?
- Would you have stuck around and investigated? Would you have tried to see what was there, or would you have tried to feel into its energy more?
- Would you ever return to a place where you felt something so strange and uncomfortable? Why, or why not?

Journal Prompts – After the Experience

- Were you able to identify any special bubble-like places in Nature?
- Were you able to distract your mind so you could more easily receive the energy?

- Were you able to easily feel when it was time to move on? What was the signal that you got?
- Do you feel like you have to do something special or important when you sit in places that feel like an energy bubble, or are you content to simply sit there and do whatever you feel like?

~

The Four Knights

Bring the learnings from previous lifetimes into this lifetime. First, become aware that this is possible. Next, set the intention to do so. Ask for help from Nature, or from whatever higher power you recognize, or from the beings around you, including Nature spirits, angels, or whomever you choose. Remember to give thanks for the help you receive.

Slow down and connect with yourself. Set the intention to connect with all the multilayered dimensions of yourself across all your lifetimes.

Journal Prompts – Before the Experience

- Do you believe in the possibility of past lifetimes? If not, why not? What do you believe instead?
- If so, do you believe that you can bring everything you've learned from past lives into your current life?
- Are you willing to set the intention to bring that

knowledge and wisdom into this current lifetime?
- How do you think it would change your life if you could remember all the wisdom that you have accumulated throughout numerous lifetimes?
- Do you think that having this knowledge would lead you to make different decisions in life?
- How do you think it might change the way you feel about things?

Journal Prompts – After the Experience

- Did you ask for help from a higher power to make it easier for you to bring the learnings from past lives into your current life? If so, which one?
- Has anything shifted in your life since trying this? Have you felt any changes? Received any insights?
- What can you do on an ongoing basis to try to bring into this lifetime your wisdom and knowledge from previous lifetimes?

Twin Sycamores

Pay attention to the seasons and observe the changes you see in Nature.

Know that there is a time and there is a place for everything. Learn to balance *wanting*, setting goals, taking action, and planning with *trusting* that everything will happen at the perfect time for you and that you will have the perfect experiences for you.

Pay attention to the things you want to experience in your life and know and trust that the best things will come to you at the best possible time. Take action toward the things that you want and be open to new experiences coming to you.

Relax and flow through unexpected changes. Expect the unexpected, and appreciate each and every experience.

Journal Prompts – Before the Experience

- Do you believe in the concept of Divine timing?
- Are you good at relaxing and flowing through the ups and downs of life?
- If so, how do you think this benefits you?
- If not, how do you think your life might be different if you did allow yourself to relax and flow? Do you think it might make things easier?
- When you look back over the years of your life, can you see how everything fell into place, even if it didn't make sense at the time?
- Can you see how things that were difficult or painful actually taught you valuable life lessons?
- If not, are you willing to spend some time now looking for what those lessons might be?

Journal Prompts – After the Experience

- What have you learned from paying attention to

the seasons and observing the changes throughout the year?

- Has it helped you to be more accepting of unexpected changes in your life?
- Has it helped you to flow through the cycles of your own life?
- Do you trust that things will come to you with the best possible timing, even though it may not be the timing you prefer?

The Somerset Four

Be spontaneous when interacting with the trees. Do whatever you feel drawn to do, whatever you feel you need: sit against the tree, hug the tree, whatever. Relax and receive. Feel whatever it is you are giving the tree and receiving from the tree. Relax and connect. Spend some time engaging with the tree, feeling into the tree. Remember to give thanks to the trees for the experience.

Allow yourself integration time for what you have received.

Journal Prompts – Before the Experience

- Do you experience ebbs and flows of doing inner work, or do you experience this in other areas of your life?
- Are you aware of the cycles in your life?
- Are there times when you feel really drawn to

spend more time in Nature, and times when you don't?
- What are the times of the year that you prefer to be outdoors?

Journal Prompts – After the Experience

- Were you able to allow yourself to be spontaneous when interacting with the trees?
- How did you choose to engage with them?
- Were you able to allow yourself to relax and receive?
- Did you feel a sense of give and take with the tree?
- How did you feel while doing this activity?
- Did you notice if you were tired, hungry, or thirsty afterward?
- Did you remember to allow yourself integration time for the energy, wisdom, or whatever it was that you received from the tree?
- How has this activity changed how you engage with Nature in general?

Railway Oak

Become aware of where you are in the cycles and the turning of the year: you may feel the need to go within in the winter, or spend more time outdoors in the spring, or be more active in the summer. Balance doing with being; action with rest.

Be present in today: journal at various points throughout the day, or in the morning, or at the end of the day, to reflect on your experience of just being in today.

Be grateful for what you have today. Be thankful for who you are today. Give gratitude for what you are doing today, for what you are capable of doing, for what you are able to do. Be thankful for having the time and the space in your life to do the things that you are doing today.

Pay attention to how this practice affects your life. Look at what has changed as a result of this experience, and then decide whether you want to experience it again.

Journal Prompts – Before the Experience

- Do you find it easy to focus on *today*, or do you find it difficult?
- Do you ever journal on what happens to you each day?
- How do you think that journaling about each day might be beneficial to your life?
- If you do not currently engage in this practice, is this something that you might be willing to try?

Journal Prompts – After the Experience

- If you gave this experience a try, how did it affect your life? What things did you notice?
- What changed in your life as a result of doing this work?
- Is it something you want to continue?
- Do you ever do gratitude work? If not, would you like to try it?

- If you engage in gratitude work, how has it changed your life? What's different for you?

Beare Green Oak

Recognize that things require time and space; give yourself the time and space you need to do the things you want to achieve. Understand that *stillness* time can be every bit as productive as *doing* time.

Give yourself space: alone time or self-care time, in which you can be quiet and be still and relax and receive and connect. Give yourself time and space *without* any sensory input (such as guided meditations, though there is a time and space for those). Consider visiting a floatation tank or meditating in a completely dark place.

Journal Prompts – Before the Experience

- Do you find it easy to sit in stillness, or is it a challenge for you?
- If it's something you find difficult, what are some ways you could add a bit of stillness to your life, even if it's just a few minutes?
- When would be a good time of day to do this?
- Do you make self-care a priority?
- What kinds of things help you to feel like you're caring for yourself? Reading a book? Taking a bath? Sitting in the garden?
- Do you get enough self-care time in your life?

- If not, when can you add a bit of self-care to your life, even if it's just a few minutes?

Journal Prompts – After the Experience

- If you have tried making stillness a part of your life, is this something you would you like to continue?
- Would you like to do it more often? Or for longer periods of time?
- What activities would you add to your self-care routine?

Wolvens Lane Beech

Take time out of each day, in the morning, in the afternoon, or in the evening, to do a daily review: spend some time reflecting or journaling. Focus on the steps that you took on your life's path on this day. What these steps gave you, what they did for you, how you felt about them, and how they contributed to your overall journey.

Journal Prompts – Before the Experience

- Do you find it easy to focus on the journey, or are you so focused on the end result that you forget to enjoy the path to get there?
- What can you do to truly relish each step of your journey?
- What can you do to enjoy each step on your path to achieve your goals?

- How do you feel about doing a daily review where you write about your day and how it contributed to your journey in life?
- How do you think that might change your life?
- When would be a good time to do this?

Journal Prompts – After the Experience

- If you tried doing this daily review as it relates to your life's journey, what did it give you?
- What new things did you become aware of as a result of doing this work?
- How did it make you feel?
- Is this something you would like to continue?

~

Newlands Corner Yew

Share the message with others of your experience of reading this book and of connecting with Nature.

Build relationships: any stories that you can tell people about building relationships with Nature will help others to build a relationship with Nature.

Be grateful for all that you receive: remember to give thanks to Nature, to the plant realm, to the trees for your experiences and for the help that they give you. Whenever you ask for help, always be sure to give thanks.

Journal Prompts – After the Experience

- What have you learned from experimenting with these different ways of connecting with the trees?
- What have you learned from spending more time in Nature and actually connecting with the trees?
- How has your life changed?
- Do you feel that it's deepened your connection with yourself?
- What would you tell a friend who was interested in spending more time in Nature?
- What stories of your own would you tell them? What experiences would you share?
- What other ways would you like to engage with Nature?
- Would you like to spend more time in Nature? How can you make this happen?

2

RESOURCES

Learn to Channel

- Cara Wilde's Channel Your Guide online course https://carawilde.com/channel-your-guide/
- Opening to Channel: Connecting with Your Guide Audio Course by Sanaya Roman and Duane Packer http://www.hollyworton.com/openingtochannel
- Lisa Wechtenhiser's WooWoo 101 online course http://www.hollyworton.com/woowoo101

Recommended Books

- *Discover Your Soul's Path Through the Akashic Records: Taking Your Life from Ordinary to ExtraOrdinary* by Linda Howe
- *Healing Through the Akashic Records: Using the*

Power of Your Sacred Wounds to Discover Your Soul's Perfection by Linda Howe
- *How to Read the Akashic Records: Accessing the Archive of the Soul and Its Journey* by Linda Howe
- *Opening to Channel: How to Connect with Your Guide* by Sanaya Roman and Duane Packer

Recommended Websites

- Chalice Well Trust Gardens: http://www.chalicewell.org.uk
- Forest Bathing and Nature Therapy Meetup: http://www.hollyworton.com/fbmeetup
- Geocaching: https://www.geocaching.com
- Megalithic, for sacred wells and sites in the UK: http://megalithic.co.uk/
- Peper Harow: http://www.peperharow.info
- Weekly Messages from your Record Keepers with Vickie Young: http://www.hollyworton.com/weeklymessages
- The Order of Bards, Ovates & Druids: https://www.druidry.org/
- Anima Monday, a blog about animism: https://animamonday.wordpress.com/

3

LEARN MORE

If you'd like to further the development of your relationship with yourself by connecting with Nature, I'd love to help you with this! Please my website to learn more: http://hollyworton.com. That's also the best place to find my latest blog posts and podcast episodes.

My primary way of supporting people at this time is through Patreon. By joining my online community there, you can receive the benefits of my done-for-you mindset work, get discounts on one-to-one sessions with me, and get free tickets to my guided Nature walks: http://www.patreon.com/hollyworton.

I occasionally run guided walks in Surrey, and I have also organized what I call woodland experience days, where I take groups out into Nature to meditate and connect with the trees. I will also be planning a series of walks that include visits to some of the trees in this book. Information on all of my events can be found on my website: http://

hollyworton.com. Admission to my walks is free for my Patrons at certain tiers.

4

GLOSSARY

Akashic Records

The Akashic Records are an extensive library of energetic records of all souls, including their past lives, present lives, and future lives. It includes all events, thoughts, words, emotions, and intentions ever to have occurred in the past, present, or futures. It is thought that each soul has its own Records, like a set of encyclopedias where each book in the set represents a single lifetime.

Channeling

Channeling involves opening up a connection or line of communication, often with unseen or nonphysical beings such as spirit guides, angels, or ascended masters. You can channel your Higher Self, and you can also channel Nature spirits, such as the spirits of the trees who shared their stories in this book.

Cloutie tree

Also known as a clootie tree or a cloughtie tree, this is a tree that has been adorned with rags or ribbons by people as they say a wish or prayer. These trees are often found near sacred wells, where people may dip the cloutie into the water before tying it to the tree. Any type of tree can be used, though hawthorns are commonly used for this purpose.

Elementals

Nature spirits. The four main types of elementals are gnomes, undines, sylphs, and salamanders, which correspond to the four elements of earth, water, air, and fire. Some consider the Fey (see below) to fall under the category of elementals.

Fey

Fairy, faerie, fair folk, fata, fay, fae. Magical creatures of Nature, or Nature spirits, often associated with forests and woodland.

Geocaching

Geocaching is an outdoor adventure game where participants use a portable GPS device or the Geocaching app on their phone to navigate to a geocache, which is a small container that has been hidden for this purpose. While urban Geocaches exist, many of them are located in Nature. There are millions of geocaches all over the world.

Multidimensional self

This is something that I've struggled to define, as online definitions never feel quite right to me. The multidimensional self is a number of things: our conscious mind, our subconscious mind, our superconscious mind — or Higher Self. It's also all the different versions of ourselves that exist in parallel universes. And as Sara O'Dowd recently explained to me, we have other versions of ourselves: an elemental version, a star being version, etc.

Tree spirits

In the same way that humans have a spirit or a soul, so do trees. It is the spirits of the trees who have told the stories of this book.

Wheel of the Year

The annual cycle or calendar of seasonal festivals which is observed by many pagans, which consists of eight festivals: the four solstices and equinoxes and the four midpoints between them: 1 February, 1 May, 1 August, and 31 October.

ABOUT THE AUTHOR

Holly Worton is an author and podcaster who helps people connect with themselves through connecting with Nature. She enjoys spending time outdoors in Nature, walking long-distance trails and exploring Britain's sacred sites. Holly is originally from California and now lives in the Surrey Hills, but has also lived in Spain, Costa Rica, Mexico, Chile, and Argentina. She is a member of the Druid order OBOD.

You can find her podcast on Apple Podcasts, or wherever you listen to podcasts. Links to subscribe, as well as the full list of episodes, can be found here: http://www.hollyworton.com/podcast/.

You can join her online community where you can receive the benefits of her done-for-you mindset work, and also get discounts on one-to-one sessions, by joining her on Patreon: https://www.patreon.com/hollyworton.

You can find her other books, including her books on walking long-distance trails and business mindset, wherever you purchased this book.

Finally, you can stay in touch by subscribing to her newsletter on her main website: http://www.hollyworton.com/.

ALSO BY HOLLY WORTON

Nature books

- *If Trees Could Talk: Life Lessons from the Wisdom of the Woods — A Companion Workbook*

Walking books

- *Alone on the South Downs Way: One Woman's Solo Journey from Winchester to Eastbourne*
- *Walking the Downs Link: Planning Guide & Reflections on Walking from St. Martha's Hill to Shoreham-by-Sea*
- *Alone on the Ridgeway: One Woman's Solo Journey from Avebury to Ivinghoe Beacon*
- *Walking the Wey-South Path: Planning Guide & Reflections on Walking from Guildford to Amberley*

Business books

- *Business Beliefs: 600+ Beliefs That Make Up a Successful Business Mindset*
- *Business Blocks: How to Identify and Release Your Blocks to Create a Successful Business Mindset*
- *Business Visibility: How to Transform Your Business Mindset & Increase Your Visibility*
- *Business Intuition: Learn to Tap Into Your Intuition*

for Easy Business Success

A REQUEST

If you enjoyed this book, please review it online. It takes just a couple of minutes to write a quick review. It would mean the world to me! Good reviews help other readers to discover new books.

Thank you, thank you, thank you.